The
Power of
Less

The
Power of
Less

The 6 Essential
Productivity
Principles That
Will Change
Your Life

LEO BABUTA

HAY HOUSE

Australia • Canada • Hong Kong • India
South Africa • United Kingdom • United States

First published and distributed in the United Kingdom by:

Hay House UK Ltd, 292B Kensal Rd, London W10 5BE.

Tel.: (44) 20 8962 1230; Fax: (44) 20 8962 1239. www.hayhouse.co.uk

Published and distributed in Australia by:

Hay House Australia Ltd, 18/36 Ralph St, Alexandria NSW 2015.

Tel.: (61) 2 9669 4299; Fax: (61) 2 9669 4144. www.hayhouse.com.au

Published and distributed in the Republic of South Africa by:

Hay House SA (Pty), Ltd, PO Box 990, Witkoppen 2068.

Tel./Fax: (27) 11 467 8904. www.hayhouse.co.za

Published and distributed in India by:

Hay House Publishers India, Muskaan Complex, Plot No.3, B-2, Vasant Kunj, New Delhi – 110 070. Tel.: (91) 11 4176 1620; Fax: (91) 11 4176 1630.

www.hayhouse.co.in

The author of this book does not dispense medical advice or prescribe the use of any technique as a form of treatment for physical or medical problems without the advice of a physician, either directly or indirectly. The intent of the author is only to offer information of a general nature to help you in your quest for emotional and spiritual wellbeing. In the event you use any of the information in this book for yourself, which is your constitutional right, the author and the publisher assume no responsibility for your actions.

First edition published in 2009 by Hyperion Books,

77 West 66th Street, New York 10023 - 6298, USA

ISBN978-1-4013-0970-1

Reprinted 2009 (twice), 2010

A catalogue record for this book is available from the British Library.

ISBN 978-1-84850-116-4

Printed and bound by CPI Bookmarque, Croydon CR0 4TD.

CONTENTS

CONTENTS

INTRODUCTION

THERE HAS NEVER BEFORE been an age in which we could get so much done so quickly. There also has never before been an age in which we were so overwhelmed with information and tasks, so overloaded with e-mails and things to read and watch, so stressed by the incredible demands of our lives.

For many people these days, work is a constant stream of e-mails, of news and requests, of phone calls and instant messages, of papers and notes and files. The day starts with an in-box full of e-mails, and ends with an in-box just as full, and each e-mail represents a request for information or for actions that we don't have time to fulfill. We are drinking from a fire hose of information, with no idea of how to reduce the flow.

It's stressful and wasteful. And if we stop to think about it, it's not how we want to spend our lives.

FINDING CALM IN THE CHAOS

What's the alternative to information and task overload? Must we follow the example of Thoreau, and build a cabin in the woods, shutting ourselves off from society and modern technology?

I propose a middle ground: one where we can still enjoy access to vast amounts of information, still have instant communication when we want it, still get things done quickly—but one in which we choose how much we consume and do. A simpler life, but one in which we accomplish the things we want to accomplish.

The solution lies in setting limits to how much we consume and do. It lies in making the most of our time by focusing on the most important things, instead of everything. Picture a life in which you have a fairly peaceful workday, where stress levels are minimal, where you're able to focus on your work. Imagine that you only do a few tasks, but they're chosen so that they have the most impact. You accomplish major goals without the stress of doing everything at once.

It might sound idyllic, but it's definitely achievable. I've done it using a system that's very easy to implement.

It all comes down to making choices.

SIMPLICITY

I'm a firm believer in simplicity. My life is better when I simplify it, when I cut down on the noise and I'm able to enjoy the things I love. My work is better when I cut out the distractions and I'm able to focus. My writing is more powerful when I can eliminate excess words and use only those words needed to convey my core ideas.

Simplicity means a lot of things in different contexts. For some, it means going back to using raw materials instead of manufactured ones, building and making everything yourself instead of buying it, doing everything yourself instead of relying on others. While that definition holds a lot of appeal for me, the simplicity I seek in my life is simplicity in what I do. Do less, not more, but achieve more because of the choices I make.

Simplicity boils down to two steps:

1. Identify the essential.
2. Eliminate the rest.

In this book, we'll talk about a lot of ways to apply those two steps to various areas of your work and personal life, but we'll always come back to those two ideas: Focus on the essential and allow everything else to drop away.

It'll make you much happier, less stressed, and perhaps surprisingly, more productive.

HOW IT WORKED FOR ME

Only a few years ago, I was over my head in debt, with a work schedule that rarely allowed me to see my family and had me stressed to maximum levels every day. I was overweight and unhealthy, I was eating fried and fatty and salty and greasy foods every day, I wasn't exercising, and I was a smoker. I was unhappy at work and going nowhere, fast. My life was complicated, and I didn't have time for the things I loved.

So I made a choice: I decided to simplify. I decided to make positive changes. It started with quitting smoking—I focused on that first, and only that. I poured all of my energy into this one goal, and an amazing thing happened: That focused energy allowed me to break through the initial barriers of quitting, which I'd failed at numerous times before.

Beating that barrier helped inspire me to new goals and habits, and I used the same method on each one: I'd focus all of my energy and attention on that one challenge, and the barriers would break down. I'd focus on one goal at a time (I call it my "One Goal") and not try to accomplish everything at once.

Through this method, over the last several years, I've been able to:

1. Take up running
2. Begin eating healthier
3. Become organized and productive
4. Train for and run two marathons
5. Work two jobs and double my income
6. Become an early riser (I wake at 4 a.m.)
7. Become a vegetarian
8. Complete two triathlons
9. Start a successful blog—Zen Habits
10. Completely eliminate my debt
11. Save a substantial emergency fund for the first time

12. Simplify my life
13. Declutter my home
14. Lose forty-plus pounds
15. Write and sell two successful e-books
16. Write the first draft of a novel
17. Quit my day job and work from home
18. Start a successful second blog, Write To Done, for writers
19. Publish this book

And I've done all of that while raising and making time for six beautiful kids.

That may sound like a lot, but I accomplished all of this in small steps, one thing at a time. Again, I used the concept of One Goal—I focused on only one goal at a time, and put all of my energy into it.

My blog, Zen Habits, which documents how I've reached these goals, is now in the top fifty blogs in the world, with more than sixty thousand subscribers and about two million readers a month. Many of my readers have asked me how I can do so much, given that I have the same number of hours in the day as everyone else. My answer: It's a matter of placing limits, and focusing on the essential.

THE SIX PRINCIPLES
OF SIMPLE PRODUCTIVITY

Part I of this book will explore the six guiding principles of the Power of Less—the ideas that will help you to maximize your productivity while simplifying your life. These Power of Less Principles will reappear throughout the book:

1. Set limitations.
2. Choose the essential.
3. Simplify.
4. Focus.
5. Create habits.
6. Start small.

In Part II of this book, the Power of Less in Practice, we'll take a look at practical tips for implementing these principles in key areas, from your work to your personal life.

WHAT THIS BOOK WILL DO

First, let me tell you what this book won't do: It won't teach you exactly how to write a novel or run a marathon or quit smoking. This isn't a how-to manual to do any of that. This is a how-to manual on how to simplify and focus on the essential. How to do less while accomplishing more. How to focus and use that focus to achieve your goals, no matter what they are.

It's about limitations rather than volume.

Each chapter of this book is designed to teach you how to focus on less and to use that focus to be more powerful in different areas of your life. You'll learn to simplify what you do, to reduce the volume of your tasks and projects and communication and information. You'll learn to reduce the clutter in your life so that you're less stressed and more productive. You'll learn how simplicity can be extremely powerful and how to use that to accomplish your goals, one at a time.

You'll learn how to create a more tranquil workday and environment, no matter where you work.

This is a book about *less*, and how focusing on less can transform your life.

And it's not an abstract book, either: It will give you very practical advice about how to put the concept of less into action, every day.

part I

the
PRINCIPLES

one

Why Less Is Powerful

WE LIVE IN a world where, more often than not, more is better. We are after more money, to buy bigger houses and cars, and more clothes and gadgets and furniture. We need bigger shopping malls rather than the small shops of yesterday. We consume more, and we produce more, and we do more than ever before.

At some point, however, we run into limits. There is only so much we can do or consume. There are a finite number of hours in a day, and once we reach that limit to our production, we can't do more. Many people see these limits as problems, while others see them as a challenge: How can I squeeze more into my day? If I manage my time effectively and learn to be more productive, can I get more done in the limited number of hours available to me?

The problem with constantly trying to increase volume is that it doesn't always produce the best results. Doing a huge number of things doesn't mean you're getting anything meaningful done. In fact, it's so hit-and-miss that it's almost like playing a game of roulette: If you do enough tasks, one of them is bound to pay off big.

It doesn't work that way. Doing more things means you're likely to do a lot of unimportant things, and you'll be overworked and stressed at the same time.

Imagine two reporters working at a newspaper: One goes for a high volume of articles each week, and the other decides to do only one. The reporter writing thirty articles a week scans a vast amount of sources for any little bit of information that's remotely interesting, turning each into a short, quick, and fairly limited article that doesn't get much attention. His editor is pleased by the amount of work he's doing, and he gets rewarded with praise.

The second reporter decides that if he's just going to do one article this week, he'd better make it count. He spends half of the first day researching and brainstorming and thinking until he chooses a high-impact story that he knows will knock people's socks off. It'll be an article that wins awards. He spends two days researching it and another couple days writing it and checking facts.

Guess what happens? Not only does he produce the best article of the week, but it becomes an award-winning article, one that the readers love and that gets him a promotion and long-term and widespread recognition. From that article, and others like it, he can build a career. The first reporter was thinking high-volume, but short-term. The second reporter focused on less, but it did much more over the long term.

That's the Power of Less.

THE LESSONS OF THE HAIKU

The fairly popular form of Japanese poetry known as the haiku has a couple of interesting lessons to teach us about why less is powerful. The haiku, as you may know, is usually a nature-related poem of just seventeen syllables, written in three lines (five syllables, then seven, then five). A poet writing a haiku must work with those limitations, must express an entire idea or image in only that number of syllables. It can be a daunting task if you have something important to convey.

So the haiku poet has a couple of choices: He can quickly whip out seventeen syllables and have a completed haiku in a short amount of time; or he can carefully choose only the essential words and images needed to convey his idea. And this second choice is what creates some of the most powerful poetry in such a limited form—choosing only the essential. So the lessons we can pick up from the haiku are the first two principles of simple productivity:

Principle 1: **By setting limitations, we must choose the essential. So in everything you do, learn to set limitations.**

Principle 2: **By choosing the essential, we create great impact with minimal resources. Always choose the essential to maximize your time and energy.**

These two lessons form the key to this book. They are the Power of Less in two sentences. Everything after this is simply an exploration of these concepts, or practical ways to apply them to many areas of your life.

CHOOSING THINGS WITH THE MOST IMPACT

In our work lives, we can be like the first reporter in the example above, cranking out tasks like crazy, and we'll probably get a whole lot done and be praised for it. People like to see hard workers who will handle anything thrown at them.

However, we can make another choice: We can be like the second reporter and choose to do fewer things, but things with the most impact. What does that mean, "the most impact"? A task or project could be "high-impact" in a number of different ways. It could:

- get you long-term recognition;
- make you a lot of money in the long run;
- be highly beneficial to your company, in terms of revenues, branding, expanding into new areas, etc.;
- change your career or have the potential to greatly advance your career;

- change your personal life in some important way; or
- contribute to society or humanity in general.

These are just some examples—you can probably think of other ways a task or project can be high-impact.

How can you determine which tasks have the most impact? There are generally two good ways of doing this.

1. **Examine your task list.** Take a look at everything on your list and ask yourself the following questions about each one: Will this have an impact that will last beyond this week or this month? How will it change my job, my career, my life? How will this further a long-term goal of mine? How important is that goal? From these answers, you can determine which items will have the most impact over the long term. While this sounds like a tedious process, it actually gets very easy with practice, and soon you'll be able to do it in just a few minutes.

2. **Start with your goals.** If you start by identifying the things you really want to accomplish in the next year, you can plan your tasks so that you are doing things each day to further those goals along. Let's say you have three long-term goals—each day, choose a task from your list that will move you closer to those goals. This will ensure that you are completing the tasks with the most impact, because they relate directly to a long-term goal.

Which of these two methods should you use? Whichever method works for you. We'll talk more about working with goals and tasks in later chapters, but for now I just want to point out that it's not an either/or choice. You can try a combination of both of the above methods, and in fact, I think that's necessary. You can do your best to plan for your goals, but even the best of us has tasks outside of those goals that must be completed. All your tasks will pile up in a long list (if you're careful to write them down) and the non-goal tasks can easily push back your goal tasks. What you'll need to do is do a review of your task list (method number one above) to choose the high-impact tasks, instead of trying to tackle everything regardless of how meaningful the tasks are to your life.

APPLYING LIMITATIONS TO EVERY ASPECT OF LIFE

The lessons of the haiku, of applying limitations in order to force choices, of choosing the essential and finding the Power of Less—these are lessons we can apply not only to the tasks on our to-do lists, but to everything in our lives. If there's any area of your life that is overwhelming you, and that you'd like to simplify, apply limitations.

Have too many e-mails in your in-box? Apply a limitation: You'll only check e-mail twice a day, and only respond to five e-mails each time. You'll be forced to work more effectively, and only write important e-mails.

Have too many projects? Limit them to three. Have too much stuff in your house? Limit yourself to two hundred items. You get the idea.

We'll explore these different areas in more detail and see how the lessons of the haiku can transform these areas of your life into something powerful and meaningful, but for now, it helps to ask yourself the following questions:

- Which areas of my life are overwhelming?
- What would I like to simplify?
- In addition to the tasks I need to accomplish in different areas, do I want to limit the number of possessions I have, what information I receive, or what responsibilities I have?

These are just preliminary questions for now; we'll explore this in more detail and figure out what's essential and what isn't as we get into the following chapters.

two

The Art of
Setting Limits

OST OF US lead lives filled with too much stuff, too much information, too many papers, too much to do, too much clutter. Unfortunately, our time and space is limited, and having too much of everything is like trying to cram a library into a single box: It can't be done, it's hard to enjoy the books, and sooner or later the box will break.

Our problem is living without limits. It's like going shopping without spending limits—you tend to go overboard and end up with a bunch of stuff you don't need or really want much. But if you have a budget (say one hundred dollars), you'll choose only the things that matter, and you'll end up with much less junk.

Our entire lives are like this: We live without limits. And while that freedom can seem fun at first, after a while it gets to be too much. We don't have enough room for everything. We can't handle the stress of trying to do everything. We just can't fit it in our lives, no matter how much we'd like to do so.

It weakens us in so many ways. It dilutes our power and effectiveness. It spreads us too thin. It tires us out so that we don't have the energy to handle the important stuff. A life without limits is taking a cup of red dye and pouring it into the ocean, and watching the color dilute into nothingness. Limited focus is putting that same cup of dye into a gallon of water.

Limitless is the pitcher who pitches nine innings every three days, throwing as many pitches as he can, as hard as he can. Soon he's too tired to pitch very hard, if at all. The real power is when that same pitcher comes in for one inning every three days and can mow down the batters every time.

Limitless is trying to excavate an entire acre of land with a single shovel. Limited focus is digging with that same shovel in one spot until you hit water.

Limitless is weak. Learn to focus yourself with limits, and you'll increase your strength. In this chapter, we'll explore Principle 1, Setting Limits.

HOW LIMITS CAN HELP

Going from a limitless life that's overwhelming and not very effective to a life with limits, focus, and power is an incredible transformation.

Here are just a few benefits of setting limits on everything you do:

- It simplifies things. Your life becomes more manageable and less stressful.
- It focuses you. Instead of diluting yourself, you focus your energy on a smaller number of things.
- It focuses on what's important. Instead of trying to do everything and not having enough time for the important things in your life, you do only what's important to you. That's an incredible change for most people.
- It helps you achieve. Many times, when we are spread too thin, we only make incremental progress on important projects and goals. But if we focus on just a few important things, we can actually complete them. You'll achieve much more by focusing on the essential.
- It shows others that your time is important. When we try to take on everything that comes our way, the people around us get the message that their time is more important than ours, that we'll say yes to whatever requests they have. If, however, we have firm limits on what we do, we send the message that we value our time and our priorities. Others will value your time in return.
- It makes you more effective. By doing less of the busy-work, and more of the important work, you are spinning your wheels less and using your limited time and energy on something with lasting impact. That helps you make the best use of your time, and eliminates much of the nonessential in your life.

LEO BABAUTA

WHAT TO SET LIMITS ON

What areas of your life need limits? Everything that you feel is in any way overloaded. Every area that you'd like to improve.

You don't need to revamp your entire life all at once. That's a sure recipe for failure, actually. Taking on too much at once is the antithesis of this book—to succeed at setting limits, you should start with one area at a time, and preferably an area with a great likelihood of success.

Where should you start? That can't be prescribed, as each person's life is different, and you'll need to do what works for you. Take a few minutes to think about your life—what areas take up too much time, or seem overloaded? What would you like to simplify? Some ideas for good places to start:

- E-mail
- Daily tasks
- The amount of time spent on the phone
- The number of projects you have on your plate
- The number of blogs or other projects you subscribe to
- The amount of time you spend reading on the Internet
- The number of things on top of your desk

These are just ideas, of course. You'll slowly be expanding into other areas. Focus on one change at a time until it becomes a part of your routine, and you're comfortable with the limit.

HOW TO SET LIMITS

When you first set a limit on something, it'll be a fairly arbitrary number, as it will take some time to see what works for you. However, setting limits isn't just pulling a random number out of a hat—it's based on your experience with that type of activity, and based on what you think your ideal is.

For example, when you first set a limit on the number of times you plan to check your e-mail, if you just randomly select a number, it could be well over a thousand. But you know from experience that that would obviously be too high a limit, so you'll likely choose from a range that's reasonable based on your years of experience in checking e-mail. Let's say you normally check e-mail ten to fifteen times a day, and that seems like too much for you. You're spending most of your day in e-mail, instead of getting your other work done. So you might choose from a range of one to five times, as that seems ideal. Maybe you'll try twice a day—once in the morning and once before you leave work.

The next step is to test it out, to see if that limit works for you. Is it a limit you can reasonably stick to? Is it hurting your communication with others in an appreciable way? Are you able to get much more work done with this limit?

Think of your first week with that limit as an experiment. If it doesn't work for you (and there's no single limit that works for everyone), then adjust it a bit. If twice a day isn't often enough, try three times a day. If you think you can get by with even less, try once a day. Then test that new limit out until you find what works for you, and until you make that limit a part of your daily routine. Once it's a habit, you can move on to the next area of your life. So setting limits for anything else will work the same way:

1. Analyze your current usage levels (how many times do you do something a day?) and pick a lower limit based on what you think would be ideal.
2. Test it out for about a week, and then analyze whether that's working for you.
3. If it doesn't work, adjust to a new level you think might work better, and test that out for about a week.
4. Continue to adjust until you find the right level and until you make it a habit.

Once you've learned to set limits, you will then learn to make the most of those limits—by choosing the essential and then simplifying. That's when the power of limits can really be seen: when the limits force you to reduce yourself to only the essentials. We'll discuss this in the next chapter.

three

Choosing the Essential, and Simplifying

IN THIS CHAPTER, we'll explore Principle 2, Choose the Essential, and then Principle 3, Simplifying. Choosing the essential is the key to simplifying—you have to choose the essential before you simplify, or you're just cutting things out without ensuring that you're keeping the important things.

How do you know what's essential? That's the key question. Once you know that, the rest is easy.

Once you know what's essential, you can reduce your projects, your tasks, your stream of incoming information, your commitments, your clutter. You just have to eliminate everything that's not essential.

It's like the old joke: how do you carve a statue of an elephant? Just chip away everything that doesn't look like an elephant. Well, first you have to know what the elephant looks like.

PUT THE HORSE BEFORE THE CART

Many productivity systems will tell you to do things in reverse: They'll tell you how to do things quickly, without trying to figure out what things you should be doing. They'll tell you how to get the urgent tasks done, and how to handle a mass of assignments and information coming at you, but these systems don't do a good job of discriminating between what's important and what's not, and you end up doing everything that's thrown at you. That puts you at the mercy of the flow of tasks and information coming at you—in other words, at the mercy of anyone's whim or requests.

Instead, you must ask yourself in everything you do, what is essential? Whether that's asking yourself what you want to do today, or this week, or this year, or in your life in general, ask yourself what is essential. Whether that be deciding which e-mails to reply to, what you can buy this month with your limited budget, how to declutter your desk or your house—ask yourself what the essentials are.

That puts the horse before the cart, instead of after it—you're identifying the essential, and then accomplishing those essentials.

CHOOSING THE ESSENTIAL:
A SERIES OF QUESTIONS

In everything you do, use these questions to guide you to choose the essential, especially if you have problems deciding.

Once you get the hang of it, you won't need these questions anymore—they'll become automatic.

1. **What are your values?** Values are simply knowing what things are most important to you. Think about the things that really matter to you, the qualities you want to have, the principles you want to live your life by. Once you've identified these values, everything you do and choose should follow from those.

2. **What are your goals?** What do you want to achieve in life? How about over the next year? How about this month? And today? If you know what you're trying to achieve, you can determine if an action or item will help you achieve it.

3. **What do you love?** Think about what you love, who you love to spend time with, what you love doing.

4. **What is important to you?** Along the same lines, make a list of the most important things in your life, in your work, or in whatever area you're thinking about.

5. **What has the biggest impact?** If you have a choice to make between a list of projects or tasks, think about which project or task will make the biggest difference in your life or career. What will have the biggest effect on everything else? For example, if you have a choice between making some calls, having a meeting, and writing a report, think about the impact each task will have: the calls are to clients who spend perhaps one hundred

dollars each on your company, the meeting is with a client who will bring in ten thousand dollars in business if you can close the deal, and the report is something that might not even be read. The meeting, in this example, has the biggest impact, and is therefore the most essential.

6. **What has the most long-term impact?** There's a difference between the size of an impact and its long-term value. For example, a meeting with a client might bring in ten thousand dollars next week, but a long-term marketing campaign might bring in hundreds of thousands of dollars over the next year. The impact doesn't have to be in terms of money—it could be anything that's valuable to you.

7. **Needs vs. wants.** This is a good criteria to use when you're trying to decide whether to spend on certain items: Which items do you actually need, and which ones are just things you want? If you can identify needs, you can eliminate most of the wants, which are nonessential.

8. **Eliminate the nonessential.** Sometimes it's useful to work backward, if you're having trouble figuring out the essentials. If you have a list of things to do, for example, start by crossing off the nonessential items. You know that washing your car, for example, isn't as important as paying your bills or fixing that leak that is costing you hundreds of dollars on your water bill. Once you eliminate some of the nonessential stuff, you are left with the more essential things on the list.

9. **Continual editing process.** Most of the time you don't pare things all the way down to the essentials on your first try. You eliminate some of the nonessentials and give the remaining things a try. Then you take another look at it in a week or two and eliminate more things. Continue that process until you are happy that you can't eliminate anything else.

HOW TO APPLY THE QUESTIONS

The list of questions above is a good way to determine which things are essential to you if you're having difficulties, no matter what area of your life you're examining. From your work projects and tasks, to e-mails, to finances, to goals, to your commitments in life, to the clutter in your home and on your desk, identifying the essentials is the first and most important step in simplifying things so that you can be more effective.

The key is to take a few moments (or hours, or days, if necessary) to stop what you're doing and think about it in a broader perspective. Are you focusing on the essentials? What are the essentials? Can you eliminate the nonessentials? Take the time to ask yourself the questions above and you'll do a much better job of honing in on what you really need to do, and really want to do—a better job of focusing on what's important, and on getting the important things done. That'll cut back on the time you spend doing things that aren't important, that you don't love doing, that don't lead to the accomplishment of your goals.

Here are some ways you can apply the essentials questions (with more detail in the following chapters on these topics):

- **Life commitments:** What commitments in your life are essential? Apply the questions above, especially those about values and goals and the things you love, to reduce your nonessential commitments.

- **Yearly goals:** At the beginning of each year, we are often filled with the desire to accomplish many goals. It doesn't always turn out the way we wanted at the beginning of the year, and one of the main reasons for that is having too many goals. Pick one or two goals for the year and focus on those. Learn to use the essentials questions to decide which goals are the most essential. You can always get to the less essential goals later.

- **Work projects and tasks:** If you have a long list of projects and tasks, you need to simplify—use the essentials questions to decide what your priorities are. What project will you focus on this week? What tasks will you focus on today? Eliminate as many nonessential projects and tasks as possible. The essentials questions regarding your goals, and the impact of each project and task, are the most relevant.

- **E-mails:** If you have twenty e-mails to answer, use the essentials questions to pick the three to five e-mails you're actually going to answer today. Worry about the nonessential ones tomorrow—or if you dare, just eliminate them.

- **Finances:** The needs vs. wants question is important here, but so are the questions about goals and values. If you align your spending with your goals and values, you'll eliminate a lot of nonessential spending, and your finances will be better off.

- **Clutter:** Eliminate clutter by starting with the needs vs. wants question, by eliminating the nonessential and using a continual editing process. Eventually you'll weed out the junk and get down to what is truly necessary and the things you truly love and use.

- **Regular review:** Choosing the essential is almost never a one-time decision. It's something you have to revisit regularly, as new things accumulate, as your values and goals change, as you learn that you can live with less and less. If you go through an area of your life and eliminate many of the nonessentials, mark a date in your calendar to revisit that area, and continue the editing process over and over. And learn to enjoy the process, not to strive for a certain destination.

Simplifying isn't meant to leave your life empty—it's meant to leave space in your life for what you really want to do. Know what those things are before you start simplifying.

Principle 3: Simplifying—Eliminating the Nonessential

Once you've identified the essential, the task of simplifying is theoretically easy—you just have to eliminate all the nonessential. However, in practice this isn't always easy, although it does get less difficult the more you do it.

Let's say you have a task list, for example, and you've identified the top three things you need to do on that list. To simplify the list, you'd want to eliminate as many of the nonessential things on the list as possible—everything that's not identified as essential. So you start by crossing off the things that aren't really important, then delegating other tasks that can be done by co-workers, and finally postponing assignments that you do need to get done but that don't need to be done today.

The hard part comes when others want you to get something done, but you don't think it's essential. In that case, you'll have to learn to say "no." We'll talk more about this in the chapter on Simple Commitments, but for now it's useful to understand that saying "no" is simply a commitment to sticking to the essentials. If that means telling people you don't have time to do more, then that's what the commitment means. And saying "no" gets easier with practice, especially as you gain confidence that sticking to the essential is something that will have great benefits to you in the long term. Additionally, others will start to respect you for being honest about what commitments you can take on without overloading yourself, and they will start to respect your time if you respect it first.

four

Simple Focus

"With the past, I have nothing to do; nor with the future. I live now."

— RALPH WALDO EMERSON

PRINCIPLE 4 of the Power of Less is that your focus is your most important tool. Focus on less to become more effective. Focus on One Goal in order to achieve it (more on this later). Focus on the task at hand instead of multitasking, and you'll be more productive. Focus on the present, to reduce anxiety and stress.

Principle 4: **Focus is your most important tool in becoming more effective.**

HOW TO USE FOCUS TO IMPROVE YOUR LIFE

Let's first look at how to use the power of focus in different ways:

- **Focus on a goal.** Focus is the most important factor in determining whether you'll achieve a goal or stick to creating a new habit. Not self-discipline, not rewards, not sheer willpower, not even motivation (though this is also an important ingredient). If you can maintain your focus on a goal or habit, you will more often than not achieve that goal or create that habit. If you can't maintain your focus, you won't achieve the goal, unless it's such an easy goal that it would have happened anyway. It's that simple.

- **Focus on now.** Focusing on the present can do a lot for you. It helps reduce stress, it helps you enjoy life to the fullest, and it can increase your effectiveness. Focusing on now, rather than the past or the future, isn't easy, and takes a lot of practice. We'll explore how to do this in the next section.

- **Focus on the task at hand.** Have you ever completely lost yourself in a task, so that the world around you disappears? You lose track of time and are completely caught up in what you're doing. That's the popular concept of "flow" (see page 63), and it's an important ingredient in finding happiness—having work and leisure that gets you in this state of flow will almost undoubtedly lead to it. People find their greatest enjoyment not when they're passively mindless, but when they're absorbed in a mindful challenge. The first step is to find work that you're passionate about. Next, you need to clear away distractions and focus completely on the task you set before yourself.

- **Focus on the positive.** One of the key skills I've learned is how to be aware of my negative thoughts, and to replace them with positive thoughts. I learned this through quitting smoking and running—there are many times when you feel like giving up, and if you don't catch these negative thoughts in time, they'll fester and grow until you actually do give up. Instead, learn to focus on the positive. Think about how great you feel. Think about how other people have done this, and that you can too. Think about how good it will feel when you accomplish what you're trying to do. Also, learn to see the positive in just about any situation. In my experience, this results in happiness, as you don't focus on the difficult or negative parts of your life, but on the good things. Be thankful for what you've been given.

FOCUSING ON ONE TASK (SINGLE-TASKING)

We live in a multitasking world. You're working on two projects at once when your boss places two new demands on your desk. You're on the phone when three new e-mails come in. You're trying to get out the door on time so you can pick up a few

27

groceries for dinner on the way home. Your BlackBerry is going off and so is your cell phone. Your coworker stops by with a request for info and your Google Reader is filled with more than a hundred articles to read.

You've learned to juggle tasks at high speed, worthy of this age of the Internet.

In these days of instant technology, we are bombarded with an overload of information and demands of our time. But we're not designed to handle this kind of overload: Soon we are so overwhelmed with things to do that our system begins to fall apart.

Instead, I advocate single-tasking, focusing on one task at a time and working as simply as possible to preserve your mental health and to improve your effectiveness. Here are a few quick reasons not to multitask:

1. Multitasking is less efficient, due to the need to switch gears for each new task and then switch back again.
2. Multitasking is more complicated, and thus leaves you more prone to stress and errors.
3. Multitasking can be crazy-making, and in this already chaotic world, we need to rein in the terror and find a little oasis of sanity and calm.

Here's how to single-task instead:

1. First thing in the morning, work on your Most Important Task. Don't do anything else until this is done. Give

yourself a short break, then start on your next Most Important Task. If you can get two to three of these done in the morning, the rest of the day is gravy.

2. When you are working on a task in a time block, turn off all other distractions. Shut off e-mail and the entire Internet if possible. Shut off your cell phone. Try not to answer your phone, if possible. Focus on that one task, and try to get it done without worrying about other stuff.

3. If you feel the urge to check your e-mail or switch to another task, stop yourself. Breathe deeply. Refocus yourself. Get back to the task at hand.

4. If other things come in while you're working, put them in your in-box, or take note of them in a small notebook or on a text file on your computer. Get back to the task at hand.

5. Every now and then, when you've completed the task at hand, process your notes and in-box, adding the tasks to your to-do lists and refiguring your schedule if necessary. Process your e-mail and other in-boxes at regular and predetermined intervals.

6. There are times when an interruption is so urgent that you cannot put it off until you're done with the task at hand. In that case, try to make a note of where you are (writing down notes if you have time) with the task at hand, and put all the documents or notes for that task together and aside (perhaps in an "action" folder or project folder). Then, when you come back to that task, you

can pull out your folder and look at your notes to see where you left off.

7. Take deep breaths, stretch, and take breaks now and then. Enjoy life. Go outside, and appreciate nature. Keep yourself sane.

HOW TO FOCUS ON THE PRESENT

Similar to single-tasking, you can learn to focus on the present, instead of the past or future, in order to stay calm, productive, effective, and sane.

The only way to learn to focus on the present is to practice. This might be hard to do at first. Your mind will wander, or you'll do a lot of "meta-thinking," which is just thinking about what you're thinking, and whether you're thinking it the right way, and whether there is a right way . . . and so on, until you're no longer in the present. That's normal. We all do that.

Don't beat yourself up about that. Don't get discouraged. Just practice. Practice in the morning. Practice while eating lunch. Practice during your evening jog or walk. Practice while washing dishes after dinner. Every opportunity you get, practice. And you'll get better. I promise.

Here are some of the best ways to practice focusing on the present:

1. **When you eat, just eat.** The best way to think about being present is this: Do just one thing at a time. When you are eating, don't read or think about something else or iron your

clothes (especially if you're eating something that might splatter on the clothes). Just eat. Pay attention to what you're eating. Really experience it—the taste, the texture. Do it slowly. Same thing with anything else: washing dishes, taking a shower, driving, working, playing. Don't do multiple things at once—just do what you're doing now, and nothing else.

2. **Be aware.** Another important step is to become more aware of your thoughts. You will inevitably think about the past and future. That's OK. Just become aware of those thoughts. Awareness will bring change.

3. **Be gentle.** If you think about the past or future, do not beat yourself up about it! Don't try to force those thoughts out of your head. Just be aware of them and gently allow them to leave. Then bring yourself back to the present.

4. **Exercise.** Exercise is my meditation. I run, and try to only run. I focus on my running, on my breathing, on my body, on nothing but the present. It's great practice.

5. **Daily routines.** Anything can be your meditation. When you wash dishes, this is practice. This is your meditation. When you walk, focus on walking. Make anything you do become practice.

6. **Put up reminders.** A reminder on your fridge or computer desktop, or on your wall, is a good thing. Or use a reminder

service to send you a daily e-mail. Whatever it takes to keep your focus on practicing being present.

7. **There is no failure.** You will mess up, but that's OK, because it is impossible to mess up. The only thing that matters is that you practice, and over time, if you keep doing it, you will learn to focus on the present more often than you do now. You cannot fail, even if you stop doing it for a while. Doing it at all is success. Celebrate every little success.

8. **Keep practicing.** When you get frustrated, just take a deep breath. When you ask yourself, "What should I do now, Self?", the answer is "Keep practicing."

five

Create New Habits, and the Power of Less Challenge

PRINCIPLE 5, Create New Habits, is the secret to making lasting changes that will actually improve your life. There is a series of habit changes recommended in every chapter of this book, but if you attempt to master all of them at once, you'll be overwhelmed and your focus will be spread out too thin. And in a matter of weeks, the changes you attempt will be for naught.

Principle 5: **Create new habits to make long-lasting improvements.**

Instead, the only way you'll form long-lasting habits is by applying the Power of Less: Focus on one habit at a time, one month at a time, so that you'll be able to focus all your energy on creating that one habit.

The tool that you'll use to form each habit is an extremely powerful one: the Power of Less Challenge, a thirty-day challenge that has proven very effective in forming habits for thousands of readers of my Zen Habits blog.

Here's how it works:

1. **Select one habit for the Challenge.** Only one habit per month. You can choose any habit—whatever you think will have the biggest impact on your life.

2. **Write down your plan.** You will need to specifically state what your goal will be each day, when you'll do it, what your "trigger" will be (the event that will immediately precede the habit that's already a part of your routine—such as exercising right after you brush your teeth), and who you will report to (see below).

3. **Post your goal publicly.** Tell as many people as possible that you are trying to form your new habit. I suggest an online forum, but you could e-mail it to coworkers and family and friends or otherwise get the word out to a large group.

4. **Report on your progress daily.** Each day, tell the same group of people whether or not you succeeded at your goal.

5. **Celebrate your new habit!** After thirty days, you will have a new habit. You will still need to make sure you do the habit each day, but it'll be fairly well entrenched if you were consistent all month.

WHY IT WORKS

This thirty-day Challenge is one of the best ways to form a habit, and it has worked repeatedly for several reasons:

- **Commitment.** Just the act of committing to the Challenge, and setting a measurable goal, and declaring it to a bunch of others, is a huge step toward making the habit change a success.
- **Accountability.** The daily check-in makes you want to do your daily habit, so you can report your success to others. There is a very positive feeling (reward) you get when you report that you did your habit today.
- **Encouragement.** There is also value in reporting your struggles. For example, during one challenge, when I got sick for a few days, I asked my group to motivate me. They were extremely encouraging, and I got back into my habit.
- **Inspiration.** When you see everyone else doing so great, it's inspiring. If they can do it, so can you! And there are always some really inspiring people in each group of challengers.

Now, you don't need to join the Monthly Challenge on the Zen Habits forums to achieve a positive habit change, but I highly recommend you find a group—online or off—to help you stick to your habit change. There are plenty of online forums and community groups to help with these kinds of things—the power of a group can help leverage your power to change a habit.

THE RULES

There are only a few rules you need to follow to make this Challenge a success. If you follow these rules, it would be hard for you not to form a new habit by the end of the thirty days.

- **Do only one habit at a time.** Do not break this rule, because I assure you that if you do multiple habits at once, you will be much less likely to succeed. Trust me—I've tried both ways many times, and in my experience there is a 100 percent rate of failure for forming multiple habits at once, and a 50 to 80 percent rate of success if you do just one habit at a time—depending on whether you follow the rest of these rules.
- **Choose an easy goal.** Don't decide to do something really hard, at least for now. Later, when you're good at habit changes, you can choose something harder. But for now, do something you know you can do every day. In fact, choose something easier than you think you can do ev-

ery day. If you think you can exercise for thirty minutes a day, choose ten minutes—making it super easy is one of the best ways to ensure you'll succeed.

- **Choose something measurable.** You should be able to say, definitively, whether you were successful or not today. If you choose exercise, set a number of minutes or something similar (twenty minutes of exercise daily, for example). Whatever your goal, have a measurement.
- **Be consistent.** You want to do your habit change at the same time every day, if possible. If you're going to exercise, do it at 7 a.m. (or 6 p.m.) every day, for example. This makes it more likely to become a habit.
- **Report daily.** You could check in every two or three days, but you'll be more likely to succeed if you report daily. This has been proven over and over again in the Challenges.
- **Keep a positive attitude!** Expect setbacks now and then, but just note them and move on. No embarrassment in this challenge.

12 KEY HABITS TO START WITH

You can choose any habits in this book that you think will help you most, at work and in the rest of your life. But if I had to recommend twelve habits to start with (one each month for a year), these are the twelve I think could make the most difference in the lives of the average person (more on each habit in later chapters):

1. Set your 3 MITs (Most Important Tasks) each morning.
2. Single-task. When you work on a task, don't switch to other tasks.
3. Process your in-box to empty.
4. Check e-mail just twice a day.
5. Exercise five to ten minutes a day.
6. Work while disconnected, with no distractions.
7. Follow a morning routine.
8. Eat more fruits and veggies every day.
9. Keep your desk decluttered.
10. Say no to commitments and requests that aren't on your Short List (see Chapter 13, Simple Commitments).
11. Declutter your house for fifteen minutes a day.
12. Stick to a five-sentence limit for e-mails.

six

Start Small

WHILE YOU WOULD do just fine if you only followed the first five principles of this book, Principle 6, Start Small, is simply a way to ensure the
greatest likelihood of success for the rest of the changes.

Principle 6: **Start new habits in small increments to ensure success.**

Oftentimes people are enthusiastic about making changes—
whether it's about implementing a new productivity system or
starting a new exercise program—so they start out with big
ambitions.

The problem is that that enthusiasm often runs out of
steam after a week or two, and the goal comes to failure. That's

what happens with almost every New Year's resolution—people start out with a lot of enthusiasm but it dies down by the end of January.

The solution is Principle 6: Start Small. Follow this principle with everything you do: with any goal, with any habit change, with any change in your life.

I've proven this principle over and over again in my life changes. When I start an exercise program, I will start with one that's as easy as possible, even if I know I can do more. When I start with a new habit, I start with just a tiny habit change, even when I think I can handle more. When I decided to start waking earlier, I started by waking only fifteen minutes earlier.

WHY STARTING SMALL WORKS

People often skip Principle 6, because they don't really understand why it's so important. Here are some of the main reasons that Starting Small works so well:

- **It narrows your focus.** Focus, as we discussed in the section on Principle 4, is incredibly important in getting anything done. If you start an enterprise or life change trying to tackle a lot at once, you spread your focus and decrease your effectiveness. But by starting small, you keep your focus narrowed, and therefore increase your power.
- **It keeps your energy and enthusiasm going for longer.** By starting out doing less than you can actually handle, you

build up energy and enthusiasm, kind of like water build-ing up behind a dam. That built-up energy and enthusi-asm ensures that you don't run out of steam early on, but can keep going for much longer.

- **It's easier to handle.** Easier is better, especially in the be-ginning. If the change you're making is hard to stick to, you are making it more likely that you'll fail.
- **You ensure success.** Choose something so small that success is almost guaranteed. Sure, a small success is not as satisfying as a big success, but it's only small in the short term. If you start out with a small success, you can build upon it, get another small success, and build upon that, and so on—until you have a series of small successes that add up to a very large success. And that's much better than a large failure.
- **Gradual change is longer-lasting.** Think of dieting—when you go on a severe, drastic diet and you lose forty pounds in two months, it feels pretty great, but more of-ten than not those forty pounds will come back, and then some. But if you do small changes—perhaps one to two pounds a week—those pounds are much more likely to stay off. This has been proven repeatedly in weight loss studies and it works with any kind of change. Make gradual changes, in a series of small steps over time, and you're more likely to stick to those changes than if you attempt a big change all at once.

HOW TO APPLY STARTING SMALL

So when and with what do you start small? Always, and with anything. Any habit change you undertake, any exercise or productivity or life change, any goal or project or task—start small.

Here are but a few examples:

- **Exercise:** Start with five to ten minutes a day, instead of thirty.
- **Waking early:** Start by waking fifteen minutes earlier, instead of an hour or two.
- **Productivity:** Start by trying to focus on the task at hand for five to ten minutes at a time.
- **E-mail effectiveness:** Start by limiting yourself to checking e-mail just a couple fewer times a day.
- **Healthy eating:** Start by making just one change to your diet, instead of doing a major diet overhaul.
- **A major project:** Start with just one small task from the project, instead of trying to tackle everything at once. Then go to the next small task, and so on.
- **Decluttering:** Start with just one drawer, instead of trying to declutter your entire office or home.

part II

in

PRACTICE

seven

Simple Goals
and Projects

I'M AS AMBITIOUS in setting goals as anyone I know—I often have several goals I'd like to achieve at work, along with self-improvement goals that can range from learning a new language to running a marathon. And while I've always been enthusiastic about setting and starting new goals, my list of things I want to achieve seems to grow faster than I progress on any of those goals.

It's easy to set goals, but extremely difficult to achieve them if they're goals worth achieving.

Tackling a goal takes energy and focus and motivation, three things that are in limited supply in any person, no matter how driven. Taking on many goals at once spreads out your available energy and focus and motivation, so that you often run out of steam after the initial couple weeks of enthusiasm. Then the goals sit there on your list, gathering dust, while you feel guilty about not achieving any of them.

The Power of Less is perfect for achieving goals: Limit yourself to fewer goals, and you'll achieve more.

At the same time, we'll look at ways to narrow your focus on your projects, so that you can complete them more effectively and move forward on your goals. We'll apply limitations to our projects to increase our effectiveness.

THE ONE GOAL SYSTEM

The One Goal System is simple—you focus on one goal at a time to increase your effectiveness with that goal. To break the goal into concrete steps, you will focus on one sub-goal at a time.

1. **Choose a goal.** Make a list of things you'd like to accomplish over the next few years. This list might have ten things on it, or maybe twenty. Now, you could try to tackle all those goals at once, or take on as many as possible. But that will dilute your effectiveness. Instead, choose just one, and focus completely on that goal until you can check it off the list.

I'd recommend that you choose a goal that you really want to accomplish—the stronger your desire, the more likely you are to actually stick with that goal until you're finished. It's not enough to say, "It would be nice to achieve this goal." You need to want it so deeply that you'll make it your top priority for months to come.

I also recommend that you choose a goal that will take about six months to a year to complete. Any longer than a year, and you will have problems maintaining your focus, and might become overwhelmed. If it's much shorter than six months, it might not be something worthy of your efforts.

What if you really want to achieve it, but it'll take two years or more? Break it down into sub-goals, so that your first sub-goal will take about a year. For example, if you want to become a lawyer, you have to get in to law school, and then complete three years of school, and then pass the bar exam. Make your first goal simply to be accepted into a decent law school—that'll take six months to a year.

2. **Break it down to a sub-goal.** Once you've decided on your One Goal, the next step is to focus on a smaller sub-goal that you can accomplish in the next month or two. In the law school example above, you might decide that your sub-goal will be to do research into some of the top law schools in the areas you prefer, to choose five schools, and to gather the essential information about each school. To shorten that, you might call this sub-goal something like, "Complete research on Top 5 schools."

The reason for a sub-goal is to create shorter steps that are more immediately achievable than a larger, yearlong goal might be. If you don't break a goal into smaller steps, you can become overwhelmed by such a large and vague goal. You can't sit down today, for example, and get accepted into a law school. It's not something that's doable. So you have to break it into more doable steps.

3. **Weekly goal.** Each week, create a weekly goal that will move you closer to your sub-goal. So this week, using the example above, you might just want to find all the decent law schools in the areas you prefer, find their Web sites, and start reading about them. That would be your weekly goal.

4. **Daily action.** Then each day, choose one action that will move you closer to your weekly goal. Make this action your most important task for the day. Do it first, before you do anything else. This will help keep you focused on your One Goal, instead of pushing it back when other, more pressing things come up.

This might sound complicated, but in action, it's fairly simple. You set a One Goal for the year (it can be set at any time—you don't have to wait for January). You set a sub-goal that will take a month or two to complete. Each week you set a weekly goal. Each day you choose a task that will move you to that weekly goal, and make that your most important task of the day.

This One Goal system will keep you focused on achieving your goal, moving closer to it each day. It will keep you from spreading yourself too thin, and will allow you to focus all your energy on completing this goal.

THE SIMPLE PROJECTS LIST

If you don't already have a projects list, I suggest you make a quick-and-dirty one right now. List all the projects you have going on in your life, including all your work projects, any personal and home projects, projects with civic organizations, and so on. Anything that would take a day or more to complete, to use a rough guideline. If you can do it in an hour or two, you can still list it if you like—a project is usually something that takes several tasks to complete.

How many items are on this list? If you're like most people, you probably have ten to twenty projects on this list. If you're an overachiever or extremely busy, you might even have more. This isn't a good thing. Too many projects leads to ineffectiveness.

Now I'm going to ask you to do something that might be a bit difficult for some of you: Choose just the top three projects on your list. Don't choose three from each area of your life—just choose three altogether.

This list of three projects is your Simple Projects List. Everything else goes on a second list, which we'll call the "On Deck List." You'll probably still get to these projects on your On Deck List, but you won't be working on them right now. They're on hold until you complete the three projects on your Simple Projects List.

Let me make this point clear: In this system I'm recommending, you don't move a project from the On Deck List to the Simple Projects List until you finish all three projects on your Simple Projects List. Not just one, but all three. Why? Because this will ensure that you don't leave one of the top three projects sitting uncompleted while you keep moving new projects onto your active list. It will ensure that you focus on completion of all of your top three projects, not just one or two.

The top three projects on your Simple Projects List will be your entire focus until you finish all three, and then the next three projects you move onto this active list will be your focus. This ensures that you aren't spreading your focus too thin, and that you're completing your projects.

I recommend that, at all times, you have at least one of your top three projects be related to your One Goal so that you are always moving that goal forward. Of the other two projects on your active list, you can choose another work-related goal and a personal goal (if you like). Whatever works best for your situation.

Why not have just one project? If limiting yourself to three projects makes you more effective, why not limit yourself to one project to make yourself even more effective? You'd think this would be logical, especially as I recommended having just One Goal. However, the reality is that almost every project is held up as you wait for information, for other people to get back to you, for others to complete tasks, for vendors or clients to do something. It's rare that you can start a project and work on it until it's finished, without any waiting. If this is possible, I suggest you do exactly that: Start a project and don't work on anything else until the project is completed.

Unfortunately, that's often not the case: We must wait for tasks or information or other things to be completed before we can move on to the next step. And so we multitask, but not on the task level—we multitask only on the project level. While one project is on hold for an hour or a day or a few days, we can be working on another. I've found that three projects works best for this type of project-level multitasking—any more than three, and you begin to lose effectiveness.

For this system to work, a project should take no more than a month to complete, and preferably only a week or two. If a project takes a year to complete (for example), then you will not be able to work on any other projects for a year. That's too long to put the rest of your life on hold. Instead, break long-term projects into smaller projects that can be completed in a month or less. If you want to launch a magazine, for example, focus first on the project of coming up with a design, then on putting together a team, then on finding financial backing, and so on.

FOCUS ON COMPLETION

Many of us lose focus of what's important when it comes to project management. We might get caught up in organizing the project, in laying out a task list and timeline, and assigning tasks to different team members. We might get caught up in meetings about our projects, in sending e-mails, and in instant-messaging people about the project. We might get caught up in the technology of it.

But the real focus of any project should be in getting it done. Completion. Each day, put your focus on moving your project forward to completion. Put aside distractions, and put all of your energy into one project at a time—you can switch to another of your three active projects when necessary, but at any given moment, just focus on one project. And move it closer to completion, until you're done.

Here are a few more tips to help you get to completion:

- **Have an outcome in mind.** How will you know when your project is complete? You should have a clearly defined outcome. Visualize what the project will look like when you're done. Then write this down in a sentence or two, next to the project title on your Simple Projects List. This is what you're working toward.

- **Move from projects to tasks.** You can't actually do projects. You can only do tasks. One of the first steps in any project, after writing out your desired outcome, is to list the tasks required to get the project to the desired outcome. Then you take this task list, choose the very next task that needs to be done, and focus on completing that task. Once that's done, focus on the next task, and so on, until you're done. One task at a time.

- **Each day, choose a task to move you to completion.** When you start your day, choose three Most Important Tasks (also known as MITs—more on this in later chapters) to complete that day. Whatever else you complete, if you complete these three MITs, you will have had a good day. At least one of those MITs should be related to one of your projects, and preferably all three should be project-related. This method will help you move your projects closer to completion each day.

- **Reassess your progress.** It's easy to get sidetracked with a project, to focus too much on organizing or communicating or technology or people. To keep yourself on track, once a week, review your projects and see how much closer you are to completion, and what still needs to be done. If you notice that you're focusing on something that's not getting you closer to completion, refocus yourself.

WHAT IF I DON'T CONTROL MY PROJECTS LIST?

If you're lucky, you have complete control over your projects list—you choose what projects to work on and the number of projects you're working on at any given time. Unfortunately, we're not all that lucky. I know the frustrations of working under a boss, where your boss dictates (sometimes to a microscopic level) what you're supposed to be working on. Sometimes bosses can be real control freaks, which might help them complete projects but isn't ideal for you.

And while you might want to limit your projects to just your top three projects in order to increase effectiveness, that's not always up to you. You might choose three projects, and then your boss might pile a few more of them on your plate and demand that they get done right away.

Fortunately, there are a few strategies you can use to limit the number of projects you're working on, even if you don't have complete control over your projects list. Not all of these strategies will work for you, but choose the one that you think will work best and give it a try:

1. **Make your own projects list.** Sometimes it's better to ask for forgiveness than to ask for permission. That means just do what you think is right, and let your boss know about it later,

after you've made it a success. This strategy works best if your boss isn't a super control freak, and doesn't demand constant progress updates. If you can work on your own for at least a few days, and preferably a week, this strategy might work. Just choose your top three projects and focus on them completely. When you've knocked them out and completed them, you can show your boss your system and point to it as your reason for success. Or don't even mention it, but keep doing it. Your boss might not care how you're completing the projects, but will probably just be happy that they're getting done.

2. **Delay.** If your boss insists that you work on more than three projects at once, and is constantly asking for progress updates, you might be successful with delay tactics. That means that you still focus on your top three projects, and try to complete them as quickly as possible—but for any others that he insists you still work on at the same time, you just delay until you can complete your top three projects. Ask for extensions, put certain tasks in other people's laps so that the project is delayed for a day or two, or just say (truthfully) that you didn't get to the project today because you were working on your other projects. I'm not suggesting dishonesty, but just honest delays.

3. **Talk to your boss about your system.** This is actually the best strategy on this list, in my opinion, and if you can pull it off, I highly recommend it. How it works: Sit down with your boss and tell him (or her) about your system—the Simple Projects List. Tell him that it will make you more effective, and that

you will be better at completing projects because of this system of limitations. Be sure that you follow through with this promise, however—your boss won't be happy if you limit yourself to three projects and then sit on them. If necessary, show your boss this book and let him read it. If that's not enough, show him my Web site (zenhabits.net) and give him my e-mail address (it's on the About page of my site). I'll talk to him.

4. **Ask your boss to choose.** If none of the above strategies work, and your boss insists on adding projects to your list and insists that you work on all of them, all the time, then you need to be honest and up-front with your boss—you only have a limited amount of time, and you can't do everything at once. Talk to your boss about this, and tell him that if he doesn't want you to choose what projects to work on, then let him choose for you. Show him the projects he's given to you, and all the items on your projects list and to-do list, and tell him you only have time to work on three projects at the moment. Let him choose which projects those will be, and tell him you will put all of your focus on completing those three projects, and that when you're done, you'll let him choose the next three, and so on. If your boss doesn't acknowledge that you have limited time, and that you can only work on so many projects at once, then you might consider looking into other job options—your boss is demanding more than is humanly possible from you.

eight

Simple Tasks

IF YOU'VE SIMPLIFIED your goals and projects (in the previous chapter), you've made great headway toward doing less but becoming more effective and more powerful. However, it's not until you get to the level of tasks that you can actually accomplish anything. You're not doing anything until you're doing tasks.

On a practical level, simplifying your tasks can be the most important step you take. As always, in this chapter we'll focus on doing less, but doing it more effectively and, in effect, accomplishing more while reducing stress.

We do that with limitations, by focusing on one thing at a time, and by focusing on small things rather than large ones.

MOST IMPORTANT TASKS (MITS)

The power of limitations works on the task level by choosing only three Most Important Tasks (MITs) that will become the focus of your day.

It's very simple: Your MITs are the tasks you most want or need to get done today. In my case, I choose three MITs each day, but you might find that only two MITs work better, or perhaps four. I suggest starting with three and seeing if that works for you.

Do I get a lot more done than three things? Of course. But the idea is that no matter what else I do today, these are the things I want to be sure of doing. So, the MIT is the first thing I do each day, right after I have a glass of water to wake me up.

What about the other things I need to do today? They're usually smaller things, not as important, but tasks or errands that need to get done anyway. Here's the beauty of MITs: Usually, the small, unimportant tasks that we need to get done every day (e-mail, phone calls, paperwork, errands, meetings, Internet browsing, etc.) will get in the way of our important, longer-term tasks—but if you make your MITs your first priority each day, the important stuff will get done instead of the unimportant.

Once I'm done with my MITs, I will do the smaller tasks in batches (I call them "batch tasks"—more on this in the next chapter).

The key to the MITs for me: At least one of the MITs should be related to one of my goals. While the other two can be work stuff (and usually are), one must be a goal action. This ensures that I am doing something to move my goals forward that day.

That makes all the difference in the world. Each day, I've done something to make my dreams come true. It's built into my morning routine: Set a task to accomplish for one of my goals. And so it happens each day, automatically.

Another key: Do your MITs first thing in the morning, either at home or when you first get to work. If you put them off till later, you will get busy and run out of time to do them. Get them out of the way, and the rest of the day, anything you accomplish is extra.

It's such a small thing to implement, and yet for most people it's a huge revelation. Sometimes small things can make big differences.

The keys to making MITs work for you:

- Set them first thing in the morning.
- Limit yourself to three.
- Ensure that one MIT is goal-related, or related to one of your top three projects.
- Focus on accomplishing these tasks above all others.
- Do your MITs early in the day, before you do anything else.
- When you do one of your MITs, be sure to single-task—focus on that task only (see Principle 4).

SMALL TASKS

Focusing on fewer but more critical tasks is important, but to really simplify our tasks we must talk about the size of the tasks as well. We can focus on just one task today, but if it's a huge and intimidating task, we can become overwhelmed and not actually do the task. Limiting our tasks doesn't get anything done if those tasks are too big.

Instead, break things down into small tasks that can be accomplished in an hour or less—even better would be twenty to thirty minutes, or even ten to fifteen minutes. The smaller, the better, because then we're more likely to actually get them done.

Let's say we have a huge task staring us in the face: "Write Annual Report." We look at that task, and we stare at it, and we know we should do it, but we stare at it some more. Then we check e-mail, or check our bank account ("My balance is still negative?"), or log on to a forum or site we enjoy, or call a friend or coworker. The large task doesn't get done.

Instead, beat that procrastination hurdle by making the task smaller. "Outline report" or "brainstorm report topics" or "write first section of report" are much better, because they're things we can do in a shorter amount of time. They're less intimidating. We can get started on them and get them done in ten to twenty minutes.

Anytime you find yourself procrastinating on an important task, see if you can break it into something smaller. Then just get started. Don't procrastinate, but just get started. Once you've gotten started, you will gain momentum, and will have broken through the initial resistance barrier, and you'll be much more likely to continue to the next small task and the next one until the large task is completed.

Small tasks are always better than large ones.

nine

Simple Time Management

THERE ARE THE super-organized among us—those who schedule every minute and stick to the plan to the letter—and then there's the rest of us. We plan our schedules, but our days don't usually resemble the plan very much.

Of course, that's because things change, and we have to be able to go with the flow. Time management, especially for the more fluid work arrangements of many people these days, doesn't have to be a rigid or time-consuming process.

Keep time management simple and avoid rigidity or complicated schedules.

AN OPEN APPROACH

For those who are overwhelmed by a schedule, and would like to take a more open approach, I suggest minimalist time management. Instead of allowing your life to be ruled by your calendar, let your life be ruled by the moment.

How can you do that? First, don't schedule appointments. This will be a radical departure for many people, but it's not a new idea and it's worked for others. If someone requests an appointment, tell them that you don't schedule appointments. Instead, ask them to call you a little before they'd like to meet to see if you can make it. If you're free, take the meeting. I suggest keeping your meetings to a bare minimum if you want to get a lot of work done. Now, there will be some things you'll want to note on a calendar (I use Google Calendar, accessible from anywhere). These are events that you'd like to have on your calendar, but you don't necessarily have to go to them. The calendar, then, serves as a way for you to see what your options are, but not as a tool to rule your life. I suggest not keeping too much on the calendar, though.

What do you do instead of keeping a schedule? Know your priorities (see the next section) and from moment to moment, decide what you should be doing based on your priorities, how much time you have available, and your energy level.

Learn to be in the moment, focusing on one task at a time, and immersing yourself completely in that task. If you aren't finding yourself passionate about a certain task, allow yourself to move on to something you're more passionate about. The more passionate you are about a task or project, the more energy you'll put into it, and the better you'll do with it.

Immersing yourself in a task, completely, is a phenomenon called "flow." Flow has gotten a lot of attention recently, in both the scientific world and the world of productivity, because people have discovered that the state of flow can lead to increased productivity and happiness. Basically, flow is a state of mind that occurs when you lose yourself in a task, and the world around you disappears. You lose track of time. We've all experienced this from time to time—the trick is learning how to purposefully get yourself into flow.

The way to get into flow:

1. Choose a task you're passionate about. If it's something you don't care about, you won't find flow.
2. Choose a task that's challenging. But not too challenging—if it's too difficult, you'll have a hard time getting into flow. If it's too easy, you'll get bored.
3. Eliminate distractions. The less you think about other things, the better. You want to focus completely on this task. Get rid of distractions such as phones, e-mail notifications, instant-messaging, clutter on your desk or computer desktop, etc.
4. Immerse yourself in the task. Just start on the task, and focus completely on it. Forget about everything else, and let the world melt away. Get excited about the task and have

fun. Warning: You may lose track of time and be late for your next appointment—which is why it's a bad idea to schedule too many appointments.

KNOW YOUR PRIORITIES

If you have an open schedule, how do you know what you should be working on at any given moment? Priorities. See the last chapter on Most Important Tasks (MITs)—basically, you should decide first thing in the morning what you want to accomplish each day. Make a short list of three things you'd really like to accomplish. Your three most important things. You can have a short list of other small tasks you'd like to do in a batch (save them for later in the day), but the focus of your day should be the list of three important things. Let this list, and not your schedule, be the ruler of your day.

Once you've set your priorities, the trick is finding focus. I highly recommend that you focus on one thing at a time. To get your short list of three important tasks completed, you'll need to focus on each one of those tasks in turn, and try to focus on them to completion. This will also be a radical departure for the multitasker in all of us. But single-tasking is not only more productive, it's more relaxing as well.

It will take a little while for you to get used to single-tasking, if you are used to jumping from one thing to another and back. That's OK. Just gently bring yourself back to your task every time you feel yourself being pulled away. Keep at it and you'll soon be knocking off your most important tasks easily.

While you're working on your task, you'll think of other things you need to do, or be interrupted by a coworker with a request, or an idea will pop into your head. You can't let those ideas and requests rule your life. Instead of switching tasks, just make a note of other tasks or ideas as they come up, to consider for later. Have a sheet of paper or a small notebook or a text file on your computer (or wherever you write your list of three important tasks), and get back to the task you were working on. When you're done with that task, you can take a look at your list to see what you should be working on next.

REDUCE YOUR TASKS

The fewer tasks you have, the less you have to do to organize them. If you focus only on those tasks that give you the most return on your time investment, then you will become more productive and have less to do. You will need only the simplest tools and system, and you will be much less stressed. I think that's a winning combination.

With task management, as with any type of organization, my philosophy is to reduce before you organize. If you only have three things to organize, instead of twenty, you actually don't need to organize. With time management, that means you should reduce what you need to do. You can eliminate tasks, delegate them, postpone them, get out of commitments. Focus always on simplifying, reducing, eliminating. And keep your focus on what's important. Everything else is easy.

BATCH PROCESSING

Aside from your three Most Important Tasks, there are always smaller tasks you need to complete each day. The trick is 1) not to let these smaller tasks take priority over your Most Important Tasks, and 2) to do them in batches as much as possible to save time. Computer programmers call this last trick "batch processing" or "batching"—you save similar tasks and then do them all at once. It saves the time it costs to switch between tasks, because instead of switching from important tasks to phone calls to e-mails to meetings to projects to phone calls again, you do all the important tasks first, then phone calls at once, all the e-mails at once, etc. Less switching means fewer complications, less time wasted, and a simpler schedule.

Make a note of these types of "batch tasks" on your to-do list, below your list of three MITs. You can group the batch tasks into different categories ("calls", "e-mails", etc.) or just have a list of "batch tasks." I highly recommend that you wait until later in the day to process these batch tasks, instead of doing them early in the day. Save the mornings for your important tasks, get them out of the way, then focus on knocking out your batch tasks as quickly as possible.

What kinds of tasks work well for batching? Here are some ideas:

- **Phone calls.** Instead of making calls throughout the day, just make a note of the calls you need to make, and do them all at once. I often reserve about thirty minutes for calls, but your needs may vary. You might also consider only receiving phone calls during a certain time—route everything to voice mail during the times you're unavailable. This will allow you to concentrate on the important tasks, rather than being interrupted every time someone feels like calling you.

- **E-mails.** This is a huge issue for most of us these days—e-mail has become so important that it can rule our lives if we let it. I'll expand on this topic in the next chapter, but basically, to batch your e-mails, just check and process e-mails at certain predetermined times throughout the day. I suggest twice a day—perhaps at 10 a.m. and 4 p.m., or whatever works best for you. Avoid doing it first thing in the morning, or you'll get so caught up in your e-mail that you'll push back your important tasks.

- **Errands.** Do all your errands at once to save the time it takes for you to go out of the home or office. You might do them at the end of the day, or save one day as your Errands Day.

- **Paperwork.** I don't have a lot of paperwork these days (I've gone paperless), but that's not a luxury for most offices. If you have a lot of paperwork you have to process or fill out or review, do that all at once rather than throughout the day.

- **In-box processing.** Similar to e-mail processing once or twice a day, in-box processing is going through the papers in your physical in-box to determine what action, if any, is required for each document. If you do this as papers come into your in-box, you'll be ruled by that, instead of being in control of your schedule. Instead, set a certain time to process your entire in-box to empty.

- **Meetings.** You might not be in control of meetings, but if you are, I recommend that you do them all at once, at a certain time, and set a very defined purpose and time limit for each meeting. It helps to batch meetings because then you have a larger part of your workday open for important tasks. If possible, avoid meetings altogether— they're most often a waste of time.

- **Different Web sites.** If you're like me, there are certain Web sites that you check regularly. Instead of letting these sites interrupt your important tasks, set a certain time to check them and do them all at once.

- **Research.** Some jobs require that you do research or reading in preparation for writing. Do this all at once if possible.

- **Maintenance.** There are little tasks that we must do as maintenance for our jobs—for bloggers like me, those are things like checking reader comments, checking or tweaking our ad systems, doing HTML code tweaks, and so on. For other jobs, there are other maintenance tasks—not your important projects or tasks, but little things that still need to be done. Batch these at the end of your day, if possible.

SIMPLE TIME MANAGEMENT TOOLS

Time management wouldn't be simple if you had too many tools, or tools that were too complicated, to manage the system. If you've followed the simple time management philosophy outlined above, you won't need a lot of tools.

Here are some simple tools you might use:

- **Calendar.** Instead of using a hefty organizer, or a complicated computer program, I recommend that you keep it as simple as possible. If you have few appointments, you might try a simple paper wall calendar—basically just boxes where you can note one or two appointments or events each day. If you have other things that need to be noted, such as your kids' soccer schedules and parent-teacher organization meetings, you might use an online calendar—I highly recommend Google Calendar, as it is simple, quick, and easy, and accessible from any computer with an Internet connection. The paper calendar or Google Calendar can also be used as a "tickler file" to mark reminders for things you want to remember later.
- **Paper notebook or text file.** I recommend a simple pocket notebook, and that's all. You can use this notebook to capture everything as you think of it, to write down your MITs and batch process tasks for today, and to write down your One Goal. If you only have one tool, you don't need to worry about it too much. If you'd prefer to use the computer to write down your tasks, I recommend

just using a simple text file. That's my current setup: I have a to-do text file, and pop it open when I need to write down a task or idea. At the top of the text file are my MITs for the day, and below that are my batch tasks, and below that are other notes or ideas that might come up. I process it once a day.

ten

Simple E-mail

FOR MANY OF us, e-mail has become one of our standard modes of working. We live in our e-mail in-box, doing everything from personal communication with family and friends to carrying out complete projects through e-mail.

Unfortunately, e-mail has also come to overwhelm us, taking us away from more important tasks, threatening to take over our lives.

There's a better way than living in your e-mail in-box. Minimize your time spent doing e-mail, transform your e-mail effectiveness by setting limitations, and become an e-mail master by getting your in-box to empty.

It's possible to do all these things, by setting limits and by learning to process e-mail quickly with simple rules and habits.

You can get out of e-mail and back to doing things that are important—your One Goal, for example, or your top three projects, or your Most Important Tasks.

The way to e-mail nirvana is by applying the Power of Less—simplify, set limits, and find yourself becoming more powerful with e-mail.

LIMIT YOUR IN-BOXES

How many different ways do you get information? Some people might have six different kinds of communications to answer—text messages, voice mails, paper documents, regular mail, blog posts, messages on different online services (MySpace, Facebook, AOL, et al). Each of these is a type of in-box, and each must be processed on a continuous basis. It's an endless process, but it doesn't have to be exhausting or stressful.

Getting your information management down to a more manageable level and into a productive zone starts by minimizing the number of in-boxes you have. Every place you have to go to check your messages or to read your incoming information is an in-box, and the more you have, the harder it is to manage everything. Cut the number of in-boxes you have down to the smallest number possible for you still to function in the ways you need to.

Here's how:

1. List all the ways you receive information. You might forget a few at first, but as you remember new ways, add them to

the list. The list should include digital and analog information—paper and computer.

2. **Evaluate each to see if it gives you value.** Sometimes we continue to check certain in-boxes, even if it's not adding anything to our lives. It's just more stuff to check. Have a pager when you also have a cell phone? Maybe the pager isn't any use to you anymore.

3. **Find ways to combine or eliminate in-boxes.** If something's not giving you value, consider eliminating it from your life. See if you can go a week without missing it. For all the rest, see if you can combine multiple information streams into one in-box. For example, how many places in your home do incoming papers get placed? Have one in-box at home for all mail, papers from work, school papers, phone notes, computer printouts, schedules, and more. Have four e-mail services? See if you can forward them all to one service. Get voice mails from a couple of different services? Try forwarding them to one service, or use an Internet service to deliver them to your e-mail in-box. At work, have one in-box for all incoming paperwork. Read a lot of blogs? Put them all into a feed-reader, in a single stream of posts, instead of having to check twenty-five different in-boxes. The fewer in-boxes you have, the better. Aim for four to seven in-boxes if possible; one or two would be ideal.

LIMIT YOUR TIME IN E-MAIL

If you spend all of your day in e-mail, or going back to e-mail and checking for new messages, you'll never get much else done. Instead, make the decision to only check e-mail at predetermined times, and leave it alone for the rest of the day—that will allow you to work on more important stuff.

I recommend that you decide, in advance, how many times you'll check e-mail, and at what times. Here are some tips:

- **Number of times per day.** How many times you check e-mail per day is a function of the kind of work you do. If you can get away with checking e-mail just once per day, that would be ideal—you'd have very few e-mail interruptions and your e-mail habits would be most efficient. However, for many people, twice a day is probably more realistic. Others, who need to be able to get e-mail more often because their job orders are sent through e-mail (customer service, for example), might want to limit their e-mail checking to once per hour (perhaps ten minutes at the top of the hour). Still others might be able to get away with checking e-mail less than once a day—every other day, twice a week, or even once a week. If you can count yourself among these people, take advantage of this and limit yourself to the bare minimum.
- **The best times.** I've found that if you check twice a day—10 a.m. and 4 p.m. are good times—that lets you get a mid-morning feel for what urgent e-mails you have

and then allows you to finish up your e-mail before you leave for the day. However, each person's workday is different—you should take a look at your work habits, your usual schedule, and your needs, and decide what times are best for you. Then stick to those times.

- **Not first thing in the morning.** A common productivity tip is not to check e-mail first thing in the morning, and it's good advice. By checking e-mail in the morning, you're allowing e-mail to dictate the rest of your day, instead of deciding for yourself what your Most Important Tasks will be for that day. You're putting yourself in danger of getting stuck in your e-mail and not getting out of it. Many people, however, have a hard time sticking with this rule of not checking e-mail first thing in the morning, because they're addicted to e-mail. While this is a common problem, it can be beat. The first step is to be more aware of your e-mail usage—pause and give some thought before actually opening up e-mail. The next step is to make it a more conscious decision—think about whether you would rather check your e-mail, or achieve your goals. If you can focus on getting your important projects done, and advancing your One Goal, instead of checking e-mail, you will be that much closer to achieving your dreams.

- **Turn off e-mail notifications.** Most e-mail programs have a way to give you an alert (through a sound or a pop-up message or a blinking icon) that lets you know you've received a new e-mail. If you use such an alert, I highly recommend that you turn it off. It interrupts whatever you're working on, and draws you back to e-mail based on the schedule of anyone who chooses to e-mail you, not at a time you determine. Instead, turn off alerts and only check e-mail at predetermined times. You'll get a lot more done this way.

- **How to stick to this habit.** It's easy to say that you should only check e-mail twice a day, but much harder to stick with it when constantly checking e-mail is an ingrained habit. How do you stick to the habit of checking e-mail less? You make it a priority for a week or two. Put up a sign with the rule: NO E-MAIL EXCEPT FOR 10 A.M. AND 4 P.M.! (or whatever schedule you choose). Every time you find yourself habitually switching to e-mail, stop yourself. Breathe. And then focus on your work instead. Your reward: You'll get a lot more done.

REDUCE YOUR INCOMING STREAM

One of the most important parts of any e-mail strategy is to stop any unnecessary e-mail from getting into your in-box in the first place. Although I get hundreds of e-mails a day, most of those e-mails never make it to the in-box. They go straight to the spam folder or the trash. You only want the essential e-mails in your in-box, or you'll be overwhelmed.

Here are some essential ways to reduce your incoming stream of e-mails:

1. **Junk.** I recommend using Gmail, as it has the best spam filter possible. I get zero spam in my in-box. That's a huge improvement over my previous accounts at Yahoo, Outlook, and Hotmail, where I'd have to tediously mark dozens of e-mails as spam.

2. **Notifications.** I often get notifications from the many online services I use, from Amazon to WordPress to PayPal and many more. As soon as I notice those types of notifications filling up my in-box, I create a filter (or "rule" if you use Mail.app or Outlook) that will automatically put these into a folder and mark them as read, or trash them, as appropriate. So for my PayPal notifications, I can always go and check on them in my "payments" folder if I like, but they never clutter my in-box.

3. **Batch work.** I get certain e-mails throughout the day that require quick action (like ten to fifteen seconds each). As I know these e-mails pretty well, I created filters that send them into a "batch" folder to be processed once a day. It takes a couple minutes to process the whole folder, and I don't have to see them in my in-box.

4. **Stupid joke e-mails.** If you have friends and family who send you chain e-mails and joke e-mails and the like, e-mail them and let them know that you are trying to lessen the huge amount of e-mail you have to deal with, and while you

appreciate them thinking of you, you'd rather not receive those kinds of messages. Some people will be hurt. They'll get over it. Others will continue to send the e-mails. I create a filter for them that sends them straight into the trash. Basically, they're on my kill-file. If they ever send an important e-mail (which is rare), they'll call me eventually and ask why I haven't responded. I tell them that their e-mail must be in my spam folder.

5. **Set expectations and publish policies.** A great strategy for reducing e-mails is to pre-empt them by letting people know not to send you certain types of e-mails, and telling them where to go for commonly requested information. As most people who e-mail me get my contact info from my Web site, I've created a set of policies published on my site that are designed to pre-empt the most common e-mails. If people follow my policies, I will get very little e-mail. For example, instead of e-mailing me to ask for a link, they can save the link for me in a popular bookmarking service. For suggestions or comments or questions, they can post them on a couple of pages that I created for that purpose. I'm also planning on creating a Frequently Asked Questions page for more common questions and issues. These policies remove the burden on me to respond to every request—I still read the comments and questions, but I only respond if I have time. My in-box has been under a much lighter burden these days. For people who don't have Web sites, they can still establish policies and a Frequently Asked Questions page by e-mailing them to other

people, publishing them on the Web, or sending out a memo to coworkers.

PROCESS TO EMPTY

So now that only the essential e-mails come into your in-box, the question is how to get it empty in the least amount of time necessary. I'm usually able to empty my in-box in about twenty minutes, although your processing time may differ, depending on how practiced you are at the following methods, and how much e-mail you get, and how focused you keep yourself. However, in any case, you should be able to get your in-box empty in a minimal amount of time using these methods.

1. **Temporary folder.** If you have a very full in-box (hundreds or thousands of messages), you should create a temporary folder ("to be filed") and get to them later, processing them perhaps thirty minutes at a time until they've all been taken care of. Start with an empty in-box, and use the following techniques to keep it empty, in as little time as possible.

2. **Have an external to-do system.** Many times the reason an e-mail is lingering in our in-box is because there is an action required in order to process it. Instead of leaving it in your in-box, and using the in-box as a de facto to-do list, make a note of the task required by the e-mail in your to-do system . . . a notebook, an online to-do program, a planner, whatever. Get the task out of your in-box. Make a reference to the e-mail if

necessary. Then archive the e-mail and be done with it. This will get rid of a lot of the e-mail in your in-box very quickly. You still have to do the task, but at least it's now on a legitimate to-do list and not keeping your in-box full.

3. **Process quickly.** Work your way from top to bottom, one e-mail at a time. Open each e-mail and dispose of it immediately. Your choices: delete, archive (for later reference), reply quickly (and archive or delete the message), put on your to-do list (and archive or delete), do the task immediately (if it requires two minutes or less—then archive or delete), or forward (and archive or delete). Notice that for each option, the e-mail is ultimately archived or deleted. Get it out of the in-box. Never leave it sitting there. And do this quickly, moving on to the next e-mail. If you practice this enough, you can plow through a couple dozen messages very quickly.

4. **Be liberal with the delete key.** Too often we feel like we need to reply to every e-mail. But we don't. Ask yourself, "What's the worst that will happen if I delete this?" If the answer isn't too bad, just delete it and move on. You can't reply to everything. Just choose the most important ones and reply to them. If you limit the e-mails you actually reply to or take action on, you get the most important stuff done in the least amount of time. The eighty-twenty rule at work.

5. **Process to done.** When you open your in-box, process it until you're done. Don't just look at an e-mail and leave it sitting

in your in-box. Get it out of there, and empty that in-box. Make it a rule: Don't leave the in-box with e-mails hanging around. Now your in-box should be empty and clean. Ahhh!

WRITE LESS

Another key to spending less time in e-mail but making the most of every e-mail you send is to write short but powerful e-mails. So after all the screening and spam filters, you've chosen the few e-mails you're actually going to respond to . . . now don't blow it by writing a novel-length response to each one. I limit myself to five sentences for each reply (at the maximum—many replies are even shorter). That forces me to be concise and to choose only the essentials of what I want to say, and limits the time I spend replying to e-mail.

Your limit might be different—perhaps a seven-sentence limit works better for you. Experiment with your limit for a few days to find your ideal length, and then do your best to stick to the limit. The key is in limitations: They force you to convey only the key concepts while limiting the amount of time you spend writing e-mails.

eleven

Simple Internet

THE INTERNET: it's not only where we get our information these days, it's where many of us live. It's where we buy things, where we meet people, where we communicate, where we play and work, where we go to waste time, where we go to do research.

With so many functions, it's no wonder we can go on the Internet to do a work task and get caught up in a dozen other sites, often wasting an hour or two before realizing it. The Internet can be a black hole of productivity, and if we let it, it can take over our lives. Apply the Power of Less to your Internet usage: Set limitations and use the Internet more powerfully. With limitations and simplicity, you can get more done both on and off the Internet.

AWARENESS: TRACK YOUR USAGE

Try this challenge: Track your Internet usage for three days. Use a tool like Toggl (www.toggl.com/), yaTimer (www.nbdtech.com/yaTimer/) or Tick (www.tickspot.com/) to track your Internet usage time, and you'll get a good picture of how you actually spend your time.

This first step helps you increase your awareness, and that's an important part of the process of getting your Internet usage under control. To simplify anything, you must first become more aware of it. And sometimes it can be an eye-opening process—we might spend a lot more time in e-mail, or at a certain site, or on the Internet in general, than we think we do.

Once you've tracked your Internet usage, you can take a look at which sites are time-wasters for you—you spend a lot of time there, but they're not helping you get to your goals. These are the sites you need to limit.

CONSCIOUSNESS: MAKE A PLAN

After awareness comes consciousness. You want to consciously plan your use of the Internet, instead of jumping on anytime you feel like it and getting carried away without thinking. Conscious use means setting limits and having a purpose to your use. That doesn't mean you can't ever use the Internet for fun, or for browsing, but you should be doing this consciously—when you need to work, work, and when you have time to play, allow yourself to play.

Your Internet plan will be different from mine, as it really depends on your needs, but here are some things to consider:

- What are your real needs? What Internet uses are critical to your work? When do you need to use these sites and how often?
- What are your fun sites? You can still use them, but limit your time on these sites. Use them as rewards for doing your work.
- When do you need to do serious, uninterrupted work, and when can you afford to browse the Internet and get distracted?

I suggest that you set blocks of your day for doing uninterrupted work (without the Internet), for doing communication like e-mail or instant messaging, for doing research and other work-related Internet activities, and for doing fun stuff or just browsing. This will allow you to be more conscious and smarter about how you use the Internet, and will allow you to get more work done.

FOCUS: LEARNING TO WORK WHILE DISCONNECTED

One of the best things I've ever done to increase my productivity is to disconnect from the Internet when I want to get focused, uninterrupted, serious work done. While I'm writing this book, for example, my Internet is disconnected. While this might sound a bit drastic to many of you who are used to being connected all the time, it's actually quite relaxing and enjoyable to be disconnected for good chunks of time, once you're used to it.

Let's say you set your three Most Important Tasks (MITs) for the day, and the first one is writing a report or a paper or an article. You might first need to do some research on the Internet, so you go on with a specific time frame (let's say thirty minutes) and a specific purpose (retrieve all the relevant info on rain forests). After you do the research, you disconnect from the Internet to write your paper or report.

Many of us have tasks like this that require research or communication on the Internet, but don't require the Internet for the main part of the task, such as writing or drawing or editing or even reading. If you do these tasks while connected to the Internet, distractions will crop up every few minutes—you think of an e-mail you need to send, or a book you want to look up, or a song you want to download. Temptations to go check on your favorite sites are constant. It's hard to stay focused on your task when the lure of the Internet is there all the time.

Disconnecting allows you to put these distractions in the background. It means you have one task to do and one task only, and it means that you'll get a lot more work done. Some tips on working while disconnected:

- Do your Internet research first, so you don't need to reconnect once you get started.

- Clear all other distractions and disconnect from the Internet so you can focus on your task.
- Set a timer and try to really focus on the task for a certain amount of time.
- When you think of something you need to do on the Internet, write it down. You can do it later. It will wait.
- Consider having an "offline hour" each day when you regularly work while disconnected. Or even an "offline day" if you think you can do it.
- If necessary, actually unplug the Internet so that you can't just reconnect with a couple clicks of the mouse.
- If really necessary, give the cord that connects you to the Internet to someone else to hold for an hour or so. Or go somewhere quiet with your laptop that doesn't have wireless Internet.
- Reward yourself for finishing your task by allowing yourself to go to some site you enjoy, but only when you're done.

You'll be amazed at how much work you'll get done.

DISCIPLINE: HOW TO STAY AWAY FROM DISTRACTIONS

The Internet, for many people, is an addiction like any other, even if we don't realize it. That means that if you try to work while disconnected, you might have a really tough time—tougher than you think. In fact, you might not even want to consider working without a connection, if you're addicted.

Like any addiction, the urge to go on the Internet can be beaten. It takes focus and energy, but it can be done. Here's how:

- Focus on breaking the addiction for at least one week. A month would be better, but I know you have other things to do. During this week, make it your goal to break free from the Internet and be able to work in disconnected mode when needed.

- Set rules for using the Internet and stick to them. Rules could include "No e-mail except at 10 and 4" or "No Internet from 9 to 10 a.m." or "No Internet in the mornings." Make up the rules based on what will be optimal for your working situation, but stick to them.

- When you get an urge to go on the Internet, let it pass. Every urge is like a wave—it builds up, then it goes away. Another wave will come, but just ride that one out too. Every urge will pass if you just wait a few minutes.

- Apply positive public pressure to yourself. Ask family, friends, and coworkers to encourage you to stay away from the Internet during the times you designate—to help you follow your own rules. Tell them to keep an eye on you, and report to them each day. This positive public pressure will help you break your addiction.

- Reward yourself. If you successfully stay away from the Internet for the time you set, give yourself a little reward—

a treat, or some time checking e-mail, or whatever will help motivate you.

- Use delay strategies that work for any addiction, such as deep breathing, drinking water, self-massage, and walking around. Do these things and the urge will pass.
- Give it some time. It takes getting used to. But the more you practice being disconnected, the better you'll get. It's a great feeling.

twelve

Simple Filing

I'VE WORKED IN several offices where people's desks were stacked with papers—one pile after another. I've had co-workers claim that the stacks are their form of organization, and yet I've seen them sifting through the piles to find a document they were sure was there. In fact, they spend so much time going through stacks that I wonder why they don't come up with a better way.

Stacking might work for some people, but for others, it's just a disorganized mess that stresses us out and creates headaches and wasted time. What is stacking, at its most basic level? It's the failure on our parts to do two things:

1. Create a simple system for organizing paperwork; and
2. Get into the habit of using that system, immediately and routinely.

Today my desk is clean and clear, simple and Zen-like—there's nothing on my desk but a phone, my iMac, and a small notebook—because I've learned to do these two basic things. Let's take a look at each one in turn.

CREATING A SIMPLE FILING SYSTEM

The key to having a usable filing system is to keep it simple. If the system is complicated or hard to use, you'll resist using it after a while. Here's how to set up your system:

1. **Reduce before organizing.** The first rule to organizing is that you should eliminate the unnecessary before organizing at all. If you've got a filing drawer that's overflowing, or stacks of paper that need filing, it'll take forever to organize—and even then, it'll be hard to find things. To simplify:

- Put everything in one big pile. If it can't all go in one pile, make more than one, but look at them as continuations of the first pile. If you have folders that are a mess, take them out and add them to the stack. I recently did this with my home filing system and reduced the files by two thirds. It took about an hour.

- Go through them, one at a time. Pick up each document or folder and decide what needs to be done with it. If you can't see yourself needing it in a couple of months, toss it. Default to toss (or shred, or recycle). Get rid of as much as you can. I've never regretted tossing a document.
- Route. If you can't toss something, and it would be better to have that item done or read by someone else, route it to that person to get it off your desk.
- File. If a document is absolutely critical, and you're sure you'll need it again, then it needs to be filed. Let's take a look at how to set up a simple system for doing that.

2. **Simple filing.** All you need is a simple, alphabetical filing system. Just use plain manila folders with labels (you can buy a label maker if you like), creating a file for each client, vendor, and/or project. I believe that most people only need one drawer for filing. There are some jobs that require much more than this, but for the average employee (or self-employed person), one drawer is all you need. And if you limit yourself to one drawer, you force yourself to toss out unnecessary files when the drawer gets full. Don't overthink this. Just create a file, and file it alphabetically. Keep it simple.

3. **File immediately.** The key to keeping your filing system up to date is to file things right away. When you're processing your in-box and you run across something that doesn't require action but that you might need to file later, don't put it in a pile

to be filed later. Don't put it in a folder labeled TO FILE or MISCEL-LANEOUS.

Just open your filing drawer (it should be close at hand), pull out the appropriate folder, put the document in it, and file it. That takes about five seconds, and then you're done. If you don't do it now, it will start to pile up, and stacking just doesn't work.

Why stacking doesn't work: It just piles up, and then the pile gets a little intimidating, and then before you know it you've got a huge pile that you never want to go through. Then you can't find anything when you need it, and now you no longer have a filing system. I know some people think that their piles are organized into a kind of system, but piles are inefficient because you constantly have to re-factor what pile is for what and which documents are in each pile, and when you need a document, it takes too long to find it. Plus, it clutters up your desk, distracting you from your work.

4. **Have materials on hand.** Always have a big supply of manila folders and labels on hand. If you have a document that needs to be filed for future reference but no file exists for it yet, you will put the filing off until later if you don't have the materials at hand. You don't feel like getting up to get a manila folder or label every time you need to file something, so you'll put it off. And that will create piles.

So instead, just have the materials in a drawer, for easy access. When you need to make a new file, just put a label on, stick the document in, and file it alphabetically.

5. Reduce your needs over time. Over the last year or so, I've consciously been reducing my filing needs so that I now barely use my filing drawer. Sure, at least once a week I'll pull open the drawer to look at a file, but I file many fewer documents than I used to. I recommend that you do the same, slowly and consciously reducing your filing needs. Here are a few tips for doing that:

- **Store reference information online.** Now when I need to look something up, I press a hot-key combination (I use AutoHotkey to open Web sites and documents) and the appropriate document opens up with all the info I need. Contacts, budget information, ideas, logs, and much more are all online, so I no longer need hard copies of them and don't need to file them.
- **Reduce incoming paper.** Ask people to e-mail you instead of faxing or sending a document by post. In this age, everything is created on a computer, and sending hard copies is outdated. Insist on digital. Also take steps to stop paper versions of newsletters, magazines, and other such regular documents.
- **Stop printing stuff.** Lots of people still print out e-mail or documents they receive, or even documents they create themselves. But then you have two copies of it, you're killing trees, and you now have to file the paper version as well as the digital. And it's much easier to search for digital information when you need it.

- **Analyze other incoming docs.** Every time you file something, ask yourself if you really need a hard copy version of it. Is it available online? Does it really need to be sent to you? Is it better to scan it and store it digitally? Is there any way to eliminate the need for this document? And slowly, one by one, reduce your need for all the incoming stuff.

HOME PAPERWORK TIPS

The five steps above can apply to both an office workplace and your paperwork at home, but here are home-specific tips for organizing all the papers in your personal life:

1. **Create one "mail center" in your home for dealing with your mail and incoming paperwork.** This should include an in-box for all incoming papers, a wastebasket (the simplifier's most important tool!), a small filing system (just some manila folders in a drawer or file case is fine), and something to hold envelopes, stamps, your checkbook, pens, and other needed tools.

2. **Home in-box.** All incoming mail, school papers, and other paperwork goes straight into your in-box. Don't toss them on a counter or the kitchen table or a desk. Put them in one place only: the in-box. It's best if you remove the mail from the envelope right away, toss the envelopes and any junk flyers, and toss junk mail and catalogs right away—but even if you don't, at least toss everything in the in-box.

3. **Pay bills immediately.** While you're processing your mail and paperwork, you can put all bills in a folder to be paid at a certain date (you might have two dates a month when you pay bills, for example, or maybe you need one day each week). But another alternative is to just pay the bill on the spot, as soon as you're done processing your in-box. Either write a check and put the bill and check in an envelope to be dropped in the mailbox tomorrow, or go to your computer and pay the bills online. Either way, the bill is taken care of and off your mind.

4. **Enter stuff into your to-do lists or calendar.** For papers that contain tasks or appointments or schedules, you'll want to enter the tasks on your to-do list immediately, and enter any dates into your calendar immediately (I use Gcal). I even enter all my kids' soccer games, school events, and other activities in Gcal, and then just file the school papers or schedules in a "school papers" folder so I can refer to it later if necessary.

5. **File immediately.** Once you've paid a bill or taken action on a piece of paper, you should file it immediately (unless you can toss it). Don't let it sit on your counter, or pile up in a "to be filed" pile or folder, or go back into your in-box. File it right away. Set up a simple filing system with manila envelopes, labeled with the name of the billing company or utility, along with folders for other important documents in your life, and use a simple alphabetical filing system so you can find things immediately. Always have a stack of manila folders and labels on hand (some people even recommend a handy Brother

label-maker) so you can create a new folder quickly if you need it. The trick to filing is to do it right away and not let it pile up.

That's it. No papers should ever be anywhere except the in-box or in your filing system. It's simple and efficient. The trick is to make this a habit, and stick to it like a routine. Have set times of the day or week when you process your in-box and pay your bills. Create a simple system like this, and you eliminate the clutter and the worry.

thirteen

Simple Commitments

IF THERE'S ONE change that you could make today that would have the biggest impact on your life in terms of productivity, effectiveness, and being able to do the things you want to do, it would be to reduce the commitments in your life.

With that one change, you could free up the time you need to focus on the important work and to achieve the things you want to achieve. With that simple change, you could free up time to pursue things you're passionate about, to exercise, to read, to find quiet time, or to spend time with loved ones.

I'm not going to lie to you: Reducing your commitments isn't easy. It takes determination, it takes a willingness to say "no," and it can take time. But it will pay off in so many ways, for the rest of your life.

THE DEMANDS OF COMMITMENTS

Most of us have lives that are overloaded with commitments. We have multiple commitments at work—besides the core duties of our job, which is already a multitude of commitments, we might also serve on different committees, have to go to different meetings, have commitments to various projects, have to go to conferences and clinics, have regular meetings with clients, or serve on boards in our industry.

Then there are civic commitments, family commitments, hobbies, stuff we have to do at home, online commitments, religious commitments, extra jobs, sports, exercise, other social groups, and more.

It's possible to have multiple commitments in all of these areas, until we have no spare time in our lives and we are worn down by the time and energy demands of each of these commitments.

Each time someone makes a request of you and you agree to that request, you're making a commitment that will take up a part of your life.

The curious thing is that we don't ever decide to do them all at once. They are added to our lives, one at a time—and viewed individually, none of them ever seems like too much work. But cumulatively, these commitments add up, so that eventually they can consume your entire life, and your life no longer belongs to you.

Cut back on those commitments, one at a time, leaving yourself with the time you need for the things that are important to you.

TAKE INVENTORY OF YOUR COMMITMENTS

In order to get a handle on your commitments, you first have to take inventory, so you know what you have on your plate. Take an inventory of the commitments in your life right now. Here are some common ones (though you may have more):

- **Work:** We have multiple commitments at our jobs. List them all.
- **Side work:** Some of us do freelance work or do odd jobs to take in money.
- **Family:** We may play a role as husband, wife, father, mother, son, daughter. These roles come with many commitments.
- **Kids:** My kids have had soccer, choir, Academic Challenge Bowl, National Junior Honor Society, basketball, spelling bee, science fair, guitar lessons, and more. Each of your kids' commitments is yours too.
- **Civic:** We may volunteer for different organizations, or be a board member or officer on a nonprofit organization.
- **Religious:** Many of us are very involved with our churches, or are part of a church organization. Or perhaps we are committed to going to service once a week.
- **Hobbies:** Perhaps you are a runner or a cyclist, or you

build models, or are part of a secret underground comic book organization. These come with commitments.

- **Home:** Aside from regular family stuff, there's the stuff you have to do at home.
- **Online:** We may be a regular on a forum or mailing list or Google group. These are online communities that come with commitments too.

You might have other categories. List everything. The more honest and complete your list, the better.

MAKE A SHORT LIST

Now take a close look at each thing on the list and ask yourself: How does this give my life value? How important is it to me? Is it in line with my life priorities and values? How would it affect my life if I dropped out? Does this further my life goals?

Then make a "Short List" of your four to five most important commitments. What are the things you love to do most, the things that are most important to you? Your list can include whatever you like, but here's mine:

1. Spending time with my wife and kids
2. Writing
3. Running
4. Reading

That's my entire list. It might take some soul-searching to cut your list down to four to five things. Once you've created your Short List, I suggest you go over your list of commitments and decide which of those commitments fit on your Short List and which don't. The commitments that align with your Short List are the essential commitments. For example, writing posts for my blog, Zen Habits, is one of my commitments. It falls under one of my Short List priorities—writing—so it is an essential commitment in my mind.

What are your essential commitments?

BEGIN ELIMINATING THE NONESSENTIAL

Everything on your commitment list that isn't essential is, by definition, nonessential. They're all on the chopping block.

Eliminating the nonessential commitments is crucial, as it will free up a lot of your time, leave you with less stress, and allow you to focus on the essential. Never have enough time for the truly important projects, or your family, or your passion in life? Now you will, if you eliminate the nonessentials and use the freed-up time for the essentials on your Short List. Here's how to eliminate the nonessential commitments on your list:

1. **Start with something small.** Don't try to eliminate everything at once. Maybe find something on the list that will be easy to eliminate. That's your first target. Look for the thing

that gives you the least return for your invested time and effort. The thing that's least in line with your life values and priorities and goals. Cut it out, at least for a couple of weeks, and see if you can get along without it.

2. **Call or e-mail to send your regrets.** Explain that you have too much on your plate right now and you simply don't have the time to fulfill the commitment. Apologize, but be firm, and don't leave any room for negotiation.

3. **Eliminate the commitment from your appointment,** and instead fill that time with something from your Short List. Don't just use that time to watch TV—use it wisely.

4. **Repeat this process** with the other nonessential commitments, one at a time, until you're done. Strive to eliminate all nonessential commitments from your list. This might take a while, especially with some commitments where you'll need to find a replacement or some other solution. But don't stop until you've eliminated all of them.

Each time you cut a commitment, it may give you a feeling of guilt, because others want you to keep that commitment. But it's also a huge relief, not having to keep that commitment each day or week or month. It frees up a lot of your time, and while others may be disappointed, you have to keep what's important to you in mind, not what's important to everyone else. If we committed to what everyone else wanted all the time, we would never have any time left for ourselves.

LEARN TO SAY "NO"

Your list of commitments didn't become overloaded by itself. Those commitments were added to your life, one by one, because you accepted them. Someone made a request and you said "yes," one commitment at a time.

Now that you're in the process of eliminating your nonessential commitments and freeing up time for your Short List, keep your list short by not adding new commitments, if at all possible. Sometimes, adding a commitment is a good thing, if it's something you love, and if you make time for it by dropping something you don't love as much. But most of the time, new commitments just add to your load and take time and energy away from more important or enjoyable pursuits.

So avoid new commitments by learning to say "no" to new requests. These requests come in all the time, at home and work, via phone or e-mail, when you run into someone at the supermarket. Learn to recognize them as requests for new commitments, and learn to turn them down.

This is very difficult for many people, who feel a sense of obligation to say "yes," who are uncomfortable turning people down, who think that they have no good reason to say no to a simple request by a friend or coworker or loved one in need.

But you do have a good reason to say "no"—a great reason, in fact: Your time is limited and precious.

You might think you have all the time in the world, and that a one-hour commitment won't matter much. But most people only have a couple hours of free time each day, when you factor in sleep and getting ready and eating time and commuting time and work and chores. Protect your time—it's your most valuable commodity. Guard it with your life.

If you have difficulty saying "no" to requests, here are some tips:

- **First, be aware.** Learn to recognize requests for what they are—demands on your time. And be aware that your time is extremely limited, and that you want to fill that limited time with the things that are important to you.
- **Consider your Short List.** Is the request in line with the four to five priorities you wrote out in your Short List? If not, the commitment is nonessential. Don't allow it to come into your life.
- **Be honest.** Tell the person that you're trying to cut back on your commitments because you've been overloaded. Tell the person that you are trying to focus and can't commit to anything new right now. Most likely, they'll understand. If not, be assured that at least you are doing what is right for you.
- **Be firm.** Say, "I just can't right now" and make it clear that you're not open to negotiation or persuasion. If you don't make that clear, they might pester you until you give in.
- **I wish I could.** Often I will honestly tell the person, "I really wish I could. It sounds great. But I just don't have the time right now." It validates the person's request but

makes it clear that you are unable to fulfill the commitment.

- **Don't be sorry.** Even if the person is insistent that you're needed for this project, don't worry—they'll find another person to fill the need. Nothing in this world has failed because one person said "no" to a request—if the need was great enough, another person filled it. So while there's a temptation to feel guilty that you're ruining something good for someone you care about, don't. That person will still get it done without you.

MAKING THE TIME FOR WHAT WE LOVE

The same concepts that you use to reduce commitments in your work life can be used to make time for what you love in your personal life.

How can we create a life where we have time to do all the things we wish we could do? Where we live a more enjoyable, relaxed life away from work? It's fairly simple, though it takes an effort to implement such a plan:

1. First, make a list of the things you truly want to do. The things you love to do. The things you want to spend your precious time doing. Shorten it to four to five things, if possible—this is your Short List, the things that are most important.
2. Eliminate as much of the rest of the stuff as possible from your private life.

3. Schedule your free time so that you're doing the things on your Short List.

It really is that simple. When I decided I wanted to spend more time with my family, it was simply a matter of making that time a priority. I would turn down invitations to social engagements, say no to friends who wanted to go out, and cancel previous commitments—just because they weren't as high a priority as spending time with my family. When I decided to run a marathon, that meant I had to get up early to run before I had to get the kids ready for school and myself ready for work. Waking earlier meant going to sleep earlier, which meant cutting back on television. No problem—running was more important to me than television. I canceled my cable TV.

When I decided to write this book, I had to cut back on other work projects, because they weren't as important. I made the time, and dedicated that time to writing. If you make the commitment to make time for the things you love by cutting out the things that are of lower priority, you can create the life you want to live. It just takes a commitment to your Short List.

TIPS FOR SIMPLIFYING YOUR PERSONAL LIFE

While creating the simple life is as simple as the three steps I outlined above, you'll get use out of the tips below. I suggest you take a weekend out of your life to examine these issues, to plan how you're going to simplify your life, and to start making changes to your schedule.

- **What's important.** First, take a step back and think about what's important to you. What do you really want to be doing? Who do you want to spend your time with? What do you want to accomplish with your work? Make a Short List of four to five things you love doing.
- **Examine your commitments.** A big part of the problem is that our lives are way too full. We can't possibly do everything we have committed to doing, and we certainly can't enjoy it if we're trying to do everything. Accept that you can't do everything, know that you want to do what's important to you, and try to eliminate the commitments that aren't as important.
- **Do less during your days.** Don't fill your day up with things to do. You will end up rushing to do them all. If you normally try (and fail) to do seven to ten things, do three important ones instead (with three more smaller items to do if you get those three done). This will give you time to do what you need to do, and not rush.
- **Leave space between tasks or appointments.** Another mistake is trying to schedule things back-to-back. This leaves no cushion in case things take longer than we planned (which they always do), and it also gives us a feeling of being rushed and stressed throughout the day. Instead, leave a good-sized gap between your appointments or tasks, allowing you to focus more on each one, and have a transition time between them.
- **Eliminate as much as possible from your to-do list.** You can't do everything on your to-do list. Even if you could,

more things will come up. Simplify your to-do list down to the essentials as much as you can. This allows you to rush less and focus more on what's important.

- **Now, slow down and enjoy every task.** This is the most important tip in this chapter. Read it twice. Whatever you're doing, whether it's a work task or taking a shower or brushing your teeth or cooking dinner or driving to work, slow down. Try to enjoy whatever you're doing. Try to pay attention, instead of thinking about other things. Be in the moment. This isn't easy, as you will often forget. But find a way to remind yourself. Unless the task involves actual pain, there isn't anything that can't be enjoyable if you give it the proper attention.

- **Single-task.** This is kind of a mantra of mine. Do one thing at a time, and do it well.

- **Eliminate stress.** Find the stressors in your life, and find ways to eliminate them.

- **Create time for solitude.** In addition to slowing down and enjoying the tasks we do, and doing less of them, it's also important to just have some time to yourself.

- **Do nothing.** Sometimes, it's good to forget about doing things, and do nothing. Don't be afraid to be lazy sometimes.

- **Sprinkle simple pleasures throughout your day.** Knowing what your simple pleasures are, and putting a few of them in each day, can go a long way to making life more enjoyable.

- **Practice being present.** You can practice being in the moment at any time during the day. Simply focus on what you're doing right now, not on the past or the future.
- **Free up time.** Simplifying your life in general is a way to free up time to do the stuff you want to do. Unfortunately, it can be hard to find time to even think about how to simplify your life. If that's the case, free up at least thirty minutes a day for thinking about simplifying. Or alternatively, free up a weekend and think about it then. How can you free up thirty minutes a day? Just a few ideas: Wake earlier, watch less TV, eat lunch at your desk, take a walk for lunch, disconnect from the Internet, do e-mail only once today, shut off your phones, do one fewer thing each day.

fourteen

Simple Daily Routine

OVER THE LAST couple of years I've discovered the power of having simple routines, especially in the morning and evening. Having these routines can supercharge your day while simultaneously creating a sense of calm and sanity in your life.

I highly recommend that you think about your mornings and evenings, as they are two key times in your day, and they can do so much to change your life. You can skip this chapter and still get a lot out of this book, but examining your daily routines is worth considering.

THE POWER OF A MORNING ROUTINE

One of the most rewarding changes in my life has been finding peace with a morning routine. I've made it a habit to wake before most others, at about 4:30 a.m., and just enjoy the quiet and solitude.

It has made all the difference in the world.

I sit quietly with a cup of coffee, and enjoy the silence. I go for a morning run, which relieves stress and is perfect for contemplation. I use the quiet time before my family awakes to write something each morning. And I read, because a good novel is one of my favorite companions.

Now, not everyone is a morning person, of course. But that doesn't mean you can't create your own routine, one that incorporates something that gives you solitude, quiet, or stress release.

If you haven't yet, I recommend that you create your own calming routine. Give it a couple of weeks to become a habit, focus on doing it every day, and soon you will not want to miss it.

With a well-planned morning routine:

- You can prepare for your day and set your goals;
- You can get in exercise, reading, writing, or other things you normally don't have time for;
- You can do something enjoyable, calming, and relaxing.

There are other things you can do with a morning routine, but those three things alone make the morning routine a very powerful tool in transforming your life.

MORNING ROUTINE IDEAS

Choose four to six of the following ideas for your morning routine—or add activities of your own. These are just ideas to help get you started. Remember to keep your routine simple. More than six things will probably be too rushed, or you won't have enough time for all of them. Test out your new routine for a few days, and make adjustments as needed. Sometimes the routine won't go as you hoped, or it will take longer than you expected. That's OK—just make adjustments.

Some ideas for your morning routine:

- Have coffee or tea.
- Watch the sunrise.
- Exercise.
- Shower.
- Take a bath.
- Read.
- Eat breakfast.
- Do yoga.
- Meditate.
- Take a walk in nature.
- Prepare lunch or lunches.
- Write.
- Journal.
- Choose your three Most Important Tasks for the day.
- Review your goals.

- Have a gratitude session (say thanks for all that you're thankful for).

Notice that "check e-mail" and other work-related activities aren't on this list. I suggest you wait until after your morning routine to get started on these types of things, otherwise you might get so caught up in e-mail that you run out of time for the rest.

SUPERCHARGE TOMORROW
WITH AN EVENING ROUTINE

If the mornings are a great time for me, the evenings are just as wonderful. Planning a calming evening routine, especially one where you prepare for the next day, can make a huge difference to your mornings.

An evening routine can take as little as ten to thirty minutes, or as long as a few hours, depending on your goals. Some common goals of an evening routine include:

- Prepare for the next day.
- Unwind from a long day.
- Review your day.
- Keep your house clean.
- Calm yourself before bed.
- Spend quality time with loved ones.
- Log, journal, write, or exercise.

EVENING ROUTINE IDEAS

Pick four to six of the following activities for your evening routine, or add ideas of your own. And again, remember to keep the routine simple, try it out for a few days, and adjust as needed.

Some ideas for your evening routine:

- Cook dinner.
- Eat dinner.
- Shower/take a bath.
- Brush your teeth/floss.
- Journal.
- Write.
- Read.
- Exercise.
- Prepare clothes/lunch for tomorrow.
- Meditate.
- Do your log.
- Review your day.
- Give yourself a facial treatment.
- Read to your kids.
- Clean up.
- Have a conversation with your partner.

Notice there's no "check e-mail" or work-related activities here either. Use the evening to relax and prepare for the next day, if possible.

HOW TO ESTABLISH ROUTINES

It might sound easy to establish simple routines, but it's just as easy to fall out of them. You want to make them a habit that will stick.

The key steps to establishing routines are to:

1. **Focus on them.** Keep your routine as your foremost goal for one month, focusing on nothing else. Having too many habits at once spreads your focus too thin, and makes success less likely.

2. **Make them rewarding.** If you establish a calming routine, the routine itself is your reward. Include enjoyable activities in the morning to start your day off right, so that you're not rushed when you begin work. In the evening, quietly prepare for the next day, review your day, and have some quiet time. Satisfying routines like that will make you look forward to doing them.

3. **Log your progress.** Reporting your progress every day on an online forum is a great way to log progress, but you could also do it in a journal or some other type of log, or put a big "X" on a wall calendar. The key is to keep track of it and see how well you've done over the course of a month.

fifteen

Declutter Your Work Space

A CLEAN DESK ALLOWS you to focus on the task at hand, which is the key to being effective in whatever you're trying to do.

We looked at a simple system that will keep all your papers in place. But what if your desk is already piled with papers—and not only papers, but knickknacks, little sticky notes, photos, mementos, tools, equipment, and more? How do you clear your desk from under the chaos? Where do you begin?

In this chapter, we'll take a look at how to begin decluttering your main work space, which is most likely your desk. We'll then look at how to use the same technique to declutter other areas of your life, including your home.

THE BENEFITS OF A CLEAN DESK

What's so great about a decluttered desk? In my experience a clean and decluttered desk has two extremely important benefits:

1. **It allows you to focus.** I've mentioned a number of times the importance of being able to focus, of clearing your desk and your mind so that you can focus on the task at hand. If you can't do that, you're losing effectiveness. And if you are working with decreased efficiency, you're wasting precious time. A cluttered desk is full of visual distractions—if you're trying to focus on one task, but glance at a pile or folder or note that reminds you of something else, you'll switch focus, at least for a few seconds. But if you clear your desk of distractions, then your mind has no choice but to focus on what you're supposed to be doing.

2. **It gives you a Zen-like sense of calm.** My clear desk helps get me into a more serene state of mind. Too much visual clutter can be stressful, even if you don't realize it. But once you clear your desk and surroundings from clutter, that stress level drops.

Given that calm and focus are two keys to this book, I think any chance to improve them is worth the effort. And if you find that you don't like this style of working, you can always go back to your old system.

HOW TO GET STARTED

Getting started is the hardest part for most people—if there are huge piles of things all over your desk (not to mention in the dark recesses of all your drawers), it's extremely intimidating. So intimidating that you never want to start.

And once you get started, you'll probably discover that it's not that hard, and for some of you it may even be fun. (It was for me.) The first step is the hardest—everything else is easy.

Here's how to get started:

1. **Set aside a little time.** You don't need to block off the whole day (though you can if you like). An hour is a good start, if you can manage it, or thirty minutes will also suffice if your day is busy. Put it on your calendar for today and don't push it back.

2. **Take all the paperwork off the top of your desk and put it in a big pile.** You'll tackle that soon.

3. **Clear everything off your desk** except your computer, phone, in-box, and other essential equipment. Everything else goes, at least for now. Put it next to the pile of papers.

4. **Start with the pile of papers**—take a chunk and start processing it from the top down. Never re-sort, never skip a single piece of paper, never put a piece of paper back on the pile. Do what needs to be done with that paper, and then move on to

the next in the pile. The options: Trash it, delegate it, file it, do it, or put it on a list to do later. In that order of preference. If you can't trash, delegate, or file it, then put it on a list of to-dos.

5. **Work for as long as you can,** then schedule another block of time when you can do another chunk of papers or other items (or when you can finish the piles, if possible).

GETTING DOWN TO THE ESSENTIALS

Once you've gotten through the piles of papers and other items that were on your desktop, it's time to ask yourself: What's essential? What do you really need to do your job? What do you use often, and what is just cluttering your work space and drawers?

Start with the top of your desk: What do you really need there on top of the desk? Ideally, this is just your working space—the stuff you need to do the task at hand, right now, not things you need later. For most people, the real essentials are a computer, a phone, an in-box (for incoming papers only), and perhaps a notebook and pen if you're like me and like to note things that need to be done later. Other than that, only the papers or folders you're using for the task at hand should be on the desktop—and when you're done with them, they go back in a folder in a drawer.

Here are some other tips for getting your work space down to the essentials:

- **If you've got folders or stacks of paper on or around your desk,** process them and put them away as in the previous section—listing them on your projects or actions lists, and filing them out of sight.
- **Get rid of distracting knickknacks, posters, pictures, etc.** A few photos of your family is fine, but if you've got a lot of other stuff, it's probably distracting.
- **Take everything out of a shelf or drawer at once.** Focus on one drawer or shelf at a time, and empty it completely. Then clean that shelf or drawer. Then, take the pile and sort it (see next tip), and put back just what you want to keep. Then tackle the next shelf or drawer.
- **Sort through your pile, one item at a time, and make quick decisions.** Have a trash bag and a giveaway box handy. When you pull everything out of a shelf or drawer, sort through the pile one item at a time. Pick up an item, and make a decision: Trash, give away, or keep. Don't put it back in the pile. Do this with the entire pile, and soon you'll be done. If you keep sorting through the pile, and re-sorting, it'll take forever. Put back only what you want to keep, and arrange it nicely.
- **Papers? Be ruthless, unless it's important.** Magazines, catalogs, junk mail, bills more than a year old, notes to yourself, notes from others, old work stuff . . . toss it! The only exception is with tax-related stuff and other important documents like warranties, birth and death and marriage certificates, insurance, wills, and so on. But you'll know those when you see them. Otherwise, toss.

- **If you are on the fence with a lot of things, create a "maybe" box.** If you can't bear to toss something because you might need it later, put it in the box, then close the box, label it, and put it in storage (garage, attic, closet), out of sight. Most likely, you'll never open that box again. If that's the case, pull it out after six months or a year and toss it or give it away.

Celebrate when you're done! Always celebrate your accomplishments, no matter how small. Even if you just decluttered one drawer, that's great. Treat yourself to something delicious. Open that drawer (or closet, or whatever), and admire its simplicity. Breathe deeply and know that you have done a good thing. Bask in your peacefulness.

A SYSTEM TO KEEP THINGS DECLUTTERED

Once you've gotten your work-space clutter to a minimum, and have created a distraction-free zone, the challenge is to keep it that way. If you go back to your old habits, it won't be long before your desk is cluttered again (usually only takes a few days).

So create a simple system and develop just a couple key habits to keep the system in place. Here's what I suggest:

1. **Keep an in-box for incoming papers.** Don't let anything get put on your desk—always put papers in the in-box, including notes and phone messages.

2. **Once a day, process the in-box to empty** using the system described in the section above—trash, forward, file, or make a note on your action list for later. Always process to empty.

3. **Have a place for each item and type of paper.** Don't allow things to pile on the desk or randomly in drawers. When you're done with something, put it in its place immediately.

Just focus on those three habits for a week—putting stuff in the in-box, processing to empty, and putting things immediately where they belong—and your new, clean desk will remain that way for months to come. It takes time to learn these habits. You'll slip. Just remind yourself, and then do it. Soon you'll have habits that will be hard to break. And trust me, once you're used to your desk being clear, you won't want to go back.

One of the things that gives me the most peace in my life is having a clean, simple home. When I wake in the morning and walk out into a living room that has been decluttered, that has a minimalist look, and where there isn't junk lying around, I start my day with calm and joy. When, on the other hand, I walk out into a living room cluttered with toys and books and extra things all over the place, my mind is chaos.

I've been a simplifier and a declutterer for years now, and I've discovered that a clean, simple home without a lot of clutter makes a big difference when it comes to your state of mind, your productivity, and your happiness. If you've got a cluttered, disorganized home, we'll look at some ways for you to conquer that clutter and keep things as simple as possible, whether you've got just a few problem areas or a huge, intimidating pile of junk.

A SIMPLE HOME

Once you've decluttered your desk, you might want to declutter your home as well. You can use the same techniques as above to declutter your living space. Just a few benefits of a simple home:

1. **Less stressful.** Clutter is a form of visual distraction, and everything in our vision pulls at our attention. The less clutter, the less visual stress we have. A simple home is calming.

2. **More appealing.** Think about photos of homes that are cluttered and photos of simple homes. The ones with almost nothing in them except some beautiful furniture, some nice artwork, and a very few pretty decorations are the ones that appeal to most of us. You can make your home more appealing by decluttering.

3. **Easier to clean.** It's hard to clean a whole bunch of objects, or to sweep or vacuum around a bunch of furniture. The more things you have, the more you have to keep clean, and the more complicated it is to clean. Think about how easy it is to

clean an empty room compared to one with fifty objects in it. That's an extreme example, of course, as I wouldn't recommend you have an empty room, but it's just to illustrate the difference.

To declutter your home, use the same steps you used above to declutter your desk, but focus on one room at a time, and within that room, focus on one drawer or shelf or other space at a time. Take everything out of the shelf or drawer, sort through it mercilessly, and just keep the essential stuff. Get rid of the rest. Then designate a home for the essential stuff you're keeping.

Set aside some time for decluttering each day—even ten to twenty minutes will do—and during that time just declutter one small area. Alternatively, you could schedule a weekend and do the entire house.

HOW TO KEEP YOUR HOME SIMPLE

Once you've gotten your house fairly decluttered, you'll want to create a system to stop clutter from accumulating. There's a reason you have tall stacks of papers all over the place, and big piles of toys and books and clothes. It's because you don't have a regular system to keep things in their place, and to get rid of stuff you don't need. You'll never get to perfect, but if you think more intelligently about how your house got cluttered, perhaps you can find ways to stop it from happening again.

Here are some suggestions for keeping the clutter from accumulating again:

- Designate a home for everything, and be fanatic. When you find stuff on flat surfaces, or draped over a chair, it might be because you don't have a designated spot for that kind of thing. If you don't, designate a spot for it immediately. If stuff doesn't have a home in your home, you need to get rid of it, or it will forever wander around the house. The other problem might be that you have already designated a spot for it, but you're just not good at putting it away. In that case, take a month to build up the habit of putting things where they belong immediately. It'll make a huge difference.

- Schedule regular decluttering sessions. Put them in your calendar. Even the best of us need to declutter regularly. If you've decluttered your home, things might be great now, but you'll need to do clutter maintenance. Put it in your calendar: perhaps once a month, once a week, or once every few months. Experiment to see what interval works for your life.

- Reduce your desires for more. If clutter is coming into your life at a rate that's too great for you to handle, you might need to look at your buying habits. Do you go shopping for clothes or gadgets or shoes or books every week (or more)? Are you always buying stuff online? If so, is it out of real necessity, or do you just like to buy stuff? It's important that you take a look at these desires, and see if you can address them. Reducing your desires will go a long way to reducing your need to fight clutter.

- Thirty-day list. This is really a way to control the desires mentioned above. Make a list: Anytime you want to buy something (other than absolute necessities), put it on the list with the date you added it. Then, don't allow yourself to buy the item until it's been on the list for thirty days. By then, your desire for that item might have passed. It's a great way to control that impulse to buy.

• Change your habits. Clutter didn't create itself. It's there because you put it there. What habits do you have that created the clutter? There may be many of them, some of them already mentioned above: You buy a lot, you don't designate a home for things, you don't put things away, you buy but don't remove things . . . You may have other habits that create clutter. Change those habits, one at a time. Take thirty days and focus on the clutter habit, and see if you can create a new habit that will reduce your clutter.

sixteen

Slow Down

THESE DAYS WE consume information, food, and media at a breakneck pace that was unimagined even two hundred years ago. We have every minute of our schedules packed with errands and tasks and chores, we rush from one place to another, we rush to get ready in the morning, and then collapse into bed at the end of a long, rushed day.

The problem is that we were not made to function this way. Our bodies and minds were made for a slower-paced life— perhaps we can handle the huge stress of being chased by a predator, but we can't handle the stresses of constant overload, and a constant hectic pace for every waking moment. As a result, we become stressed out, burned out, and unhappy. Learn to move at a slower pace and you will be happier, and just as importantly, you will become more effective and productive.

You won't learn to do more in less time, but you'll learn to do things better, and to do the right things. This simple combination can have a wondrous impact on your effectiveness, and how much you accomplish. In the meantime, no matter what you accomplish, you will be better off.

SLOW ATTENTION

Our attention is one of our most important assets. What we focus our attention on becomes our reality. The projects we focus on are the projects that get completed.

Unfortunately, with the hectic pace of our lives, our attention is pulled in a million different directions all the time. We switch our attention from one thing to the next and back again, and then back to another thing, then to a new thing. As a result, nothing gets enough attention.

Learn, instead, to focus your attention, to move it from one thing to the next more reluctantly, more slowly, at a more relaxed pace. As a result, things will start getting done. You'll start to notice things more. You'll be less stressed.

Here's how to do it:

- **Pick a simple task to start with.** Try to keep your attention on this task without switching. This could be something like eating, gardening, washing dishes, ironing, or cooking. Every time you switch your attention, take note of it. After you become more aware of your attention, learn to stop yourself when you begin to switch your attention.

- **Practice this method throughout your day, no matter what you're doing.** If you're showering, focus on your showering. If you're eating, focus on your eating (see below for more). Stop yourself when your attention wanders.

- **If you'd like to try a very restful morning practice, try a simple meditation technique** (no chanting or anything like that). Simply sit somewhere comfortable, early in the morning, and close your eyes (don't fall asleep!). Then focus your attention on your breathing. If your attention wanders, simply become aware of it, acknowledge the thoughts that come into your head, and return your attention to your breathing. Feel your breath as it comes into your body, and then as it exits. Keep your attention on your breathing for as long as possible. It takes practice, but you'll get better at it.

SLOW WORKING

Along the same lines, working at a slower pace can be more productive, as contradictory as that might sound. If you can focus on the important tasks and projects, and keep your focus on those tasks, you will accomplish important things.

In contrast, someone can work frantically for twelve hours a day, doing as many tasks as possible, and yet not accomplish anything important. That's not just theory—many people do it all the time. They work hard at a fast pace, and yet wonder why they don't get anywhere, and nothing seems to get done. They multitask and work as quickly as possible, getting stressed out the whole time. It's not the most effective way to work.

Instead, try this method:

1. **Choose work you love.** If you dread a task, you'll have a hard time losing yourself in it. If your job is made up of stuff you hate, you might want to consider finding another job. Or consider seeking projects you love to do within your current job. At any rate, be sure that whatever task you choose is something you can be passionate about.

2. **Choose an important task.** There's work you love that's easy and unimportant, and then there's work you love that will make a long-term impact on your career and life. Choose the latter, as it will be a much better use of your time.

3. **Make sure it's challenging, but not too hard.** If a task is too easy, you will be able to complete it without much thought or effort. A task should be challenging enough to require your full concentration. However, if it is too hard, you will find it difficult to lose yourself in it, as you will spend most of your concentration just trying to figure out how to do it—either that or you'll end up discouraged. It may take some trial and error to find tasks of the appropriate level of difficulty.

4. **Find your quiet, peak time.** This is actually two steps grouped into one. First, you'll want to find a time that's quiet, or you'll never be able to focus. For me, that's mornings, before the

hustle of everyday life builds to a dull roar. That might be early morning, when you just wake, or early in the workday, when most people haven't arrived yet or are still getting their coffee and settling down. Or you might try the lunch hour, when people are usually out of the office. Evenings also work well for many people. Or, if you're lucky, you can do it at any time of the day if you can find a quiet spot to work in. Whatever time you choose, it should also be a peak energy time for you. Some people get tired after lunch—that's not a good time for this method. Find a time when you have lots of energy and can concentrate.

5. **Clear away distractions, and focus.** Aside from finding a quiet time and place to work, you'll want to clear away all other distractions. That means turning off distracting music (unless you find music that helps you focus), turning off phones, e-mail, and IM notifications, and anything else that might pop up or make noise to interrupt your thoughts. Then learn to focus on that task for as long as possible.

6. **Enjoy yourself.** Losing yourself in a task is an amazing thing, in my experience. It feels great to be able to really pour yourself into something worthwhile, to make great progress on a project or important task, to do something you're passionate about. Take the time to appreciate this feeling.

7. **Keep practicing.** Again, this takes practice. Each step will take some practice, from finding a quiet, peak time for yourself, to clearing distractions, to choosing the right task.

And especially keeping your focus on a task for a long time. But each time you fail, try to learn from it. Each time you succeed, you should also learn from it—what did you do right? And the more you practice, the better you'll get.

8. **Reap the rewards.** Aside from the pleasure of immersing yourself in a task, you'll also be happier with your work in general. You'll get important projects done. You'll complete tasks more often, rather than starting and stopping frequently. All of this is hugely satisfying and rewarding. Take the time to appreciate this, and to continue to practice it every day.

SLOW EATING

Many of us rush through the day, with no time for anything . . . and when we have time to get a bite to eat, we gobble it down. That leads to stressful, unhealthy living.

With the simple but powerful act of eating more slowly, we can begin to reverse that lifestyle immediately. How hard is it? You take smaller bites, you chew each bite slower and longer, and you enjoy your meal longer. It takes only a few extra minutes each meal, and yet it can have profound effects.

Some good reasons you should consider the simple act of eating more slowly:

1. **Lose weight.** A growing number of studies confirm that just by eating more slowly, you'll consume fewer calories—in fact, enough to lose twenty pounds a year without doing any-

thing different or eating anything different. The reason is that it takes about twenty minutes for our brains to register that we're full. If we eat quickly, we can continue eating past the point where we're full. If we eat slowly, we have time to realize we're full, and stop on time. Now, I still recommend that you eat healthier foods, but if you're looking to lose weight, eating slowly should also be a part of your new lifestyle.

2. **Enjoy your food.** This reason is just as powerful. It's hard to enjoy your food if it goes by too quickly. In fact, I think it's fine to eat sinful foods, if you eat a small amount slowly. Think about it: You want to eat sinful foods (desserts, fried foods, pizza, etc.) because they taste good. But if you eat them fast, what's the point? If you eat them slowly, you can get the same amount of great taste, but with less going straight into your stomach. That's math that works for me. And that argument aside, I think you are just happier by tasting great food and enjoying it fully—by eating slowly. Make your meals a gastronomic pleasure, not a thing you do in a rushed way, between stressful events.

3. **Better digestion.** If you eat slowly, you'll chew your food better, which leads to better digestion. Digestion actually starts in the mouth, so the more work you do up there, the less you'll have to do in your stomach. This can help lead to fewer digestive problems.

4. **Less stress.** Eating slowly, and paying attention to our eating, can be a great form of mindfulness exercise. Be in the

moment, rather than rushing through a meal thinking about what you need to do next. When you eat, you should eat. This kind of mindfulness will lead to a less stressful life, and long-term happiness. Give it a try.

5. **Rebel against fast food and fast life.** Our hectic, fast-paced, stressful, chaotic lives—the fast life—leads to eating fast food, and eating it quickly. This is a lifestyle that is dehumanizing us, making us unhealthy, stressed out, and unhappy. We rush through our day, doing one mindless task after another, without taking the time to live life, to enjoy life, to relate to each other, to be human. That's not a good thing in my book. Instead, rebel against that entire lifestyle and philosophy . . . with the small act of eating slowly. Don't eat fast food. Eat at a good restaurant, or better yet, cook your own food and enjoy it fully. Taste life itself.

SLOW DRIVING

I drive more slowly these days. While I used to be a bit of a driving maniac (ask my wife), passing everybody and stepping hard on my accelerator, I would also get increasingly frustrated when people would drive slowly and keep me from driving fast, or cut me off. Driving was a stressful experience.

Not anymore. These days, driving is a much more calm, serene experience, and I enjoy it much more.

I look around at other drivers and wonder whether they really need to get to where they're going so fast, and whether they'll slow down when they get there. I wonder if it's really worth burning all that gas and getting so angry and risking so many lives. And then I think about other things, because driving for me has become a time of contemplation. I heartily recommend driving more slowly—for many reasons, but one of the best reasons is that it has made me a much happier person. It's such a simple step to take, but it makes an incredibly big difference.

Here are just five reasons to drive slower:

1. **Save gas.** The best ways to save gas (besides driving less or driving a fuel-efficient vehicle) are to avoid excessive idling, to do more gradual accelerating and decelerating, and to drive more slowly. With gas prices so high these days, wasting gas by driving unnecessarily fast is something we can't afford.

2. **Save lives.** Driving fast can kill people (including the driver). Two stats: Traffic accidents are the biggest single killer of twelve- to sixteen-year-olds. Surprisingly, at thirty-five miles per hour you are twice as likely to kill someone you hit as at thirty miles per hour. Faster driving gives you a shorter amount of time to respond to something in your path, and even a fraction of a second can mean the difference between life and death. Drive more slowly for your safety and that of those around you . . . and especially drive slowly around runners, cyclists, schools, and neighborhoods with kids on the streets.

3. **Save time?** While you think you're saving time by driving faster, it's not a lot of time. And that small amount of time

you're saving isn't worth it when you consider the other factors on this list. Better yet, start out a few minutes early and you'll arrive at the same time as someone who drove faster but started later—and you'll arrive much happier than that person, to boot.

4. **Save your sanity.** The above three reasons are very important ones, but for me the most noticeable difference has been the huge drop in my stress level when I drive. Far from being a crazy experience, driving is now actually a relaxing and pleasant experience. I no longer get road rage, because I simply don't care whether other drivers are going slowly or cutting me off.

5. **Simplify your life.** This is related to the point above, but expanded. In addition to improving your stress levels, driving more slowly can reduce many other complications—the headache of accidents and speeding tickets, for one; going to the gas station too often, for another. It can also improve the hectic pace of life. Why must we rush through life? Slow down and enjoy it more. If we're always in a hurry to get places, when will we get to our destination and finally be happy? Life is a journey—make it a pleasant one.

Here are some of the slow-driving tips that have worked for me:

- **Play relaxing music.** Anything that relaxes you is good.
- **Ignore other drivers.** This was my problem before. I cared

so much about what the other drivers were doing that it would stress me out. At times, it would cause me to drive faster to spite other drivers (awful, I know). Now I just ignore them.

- **Leave early.** If you speed because you're running late, make it a habit of getting ready early and leaving early. This way you don't have to worry about being late, and you can enjoy the ride.

- **Brainstorm.** I like to use my driving time for contemplation. I come up with ideas for things to write about, I think about my day (either the day to come or the day in review), I think about my life as a whole and where I want to go.

- **Keep to the right.** If you drive slower than the other crazy drivers out there, it's wise to keep out of their way if possible and keep to the right. While I tend to ignore other drivers who might get mad at me for driving slow (I don't care about them anymore), it's good to be polite.

- **Enjoy the drive.** Most of all, make your drive a pleasant experience—whether that's through music or contemplation or however you want to enjoy the ride, remember that the ride is just as important as the destination.

seventeen

Simple Health and Fitness

THE BENEFITS OF exercise and better fitness and health are many, but among the best of these benefits is greater energy and productivity. A good workout, for example, can leave you feeling energetic all day, and put you in a great frame of mind for achieving a lot at work. But while so many of us want to get in shape and to live healthier lifestyles, it's such an uphill struggle for so many people that they often give up in disappointment and frustration, or don't even try in the first place.

The recipe for getting lean and fit and healthy is simple, of course, and everyone knows it: Eat healthily and exercise regularly. But while those basics are well known, how to actually accomplish them, with all the difficulties we face in our everyday lives, is much more complicated.

Or at least it seems complicated if you haven't already figured it out. It doesn't have to be. In this chapter we'll first take a quick look at some of the difficulties we all face with fitness, then look at a simple fitness plan, and how to stay motivated to stick to that plan. And as healthy eating is inextricably linked to fitness, we'll look at some good ways to eat healthier as well.

THE DIFFICULTIES OF FITNESS

Let's start with why it's so hard to eat healthy for most people, and why they often fail after a week or two. From these reasons, we'll be able to come up with some simple solutions.

Some of the more common reasons:

- Their diets are too restrictive and they find it too hard to stay on such a strict diet for long.
- They starve themselves and then get so hungry they go on binges.
- They think they're eating healthily but often eat or drink lots of "hidden" empty calories, such as those in sodas or other drinks, high-fat dressings or toppings, and so on.
- The lure of junk food and fast food is too tempting, especially when they're on the road, busy at work, or otherwise in a hurry.
- Social situations, such as office parties, family get-togethers, nights out with friends, anniversary dinners, and the like often sabotage an otherwise healthy diet.

Those five reasons alone will cause almost anyone to stray from healthy eating if they don't properly prepare themselves and come up with a plan that can survive everyday life for longer than a month or two.

Sticking to an exercise program can be just as difficult, and a good program will take into account these difficulties. Here are some of the more common reasons people have trouble with exercise:

- They start out with a very challenging program or increase the difficulty of their workouts rapidly, and then burn out quickly or get injured.
- They don't see results after a week or two and lose motivation.
- Life gets in the way, and they don't find time to work out for a few days, and fall out of the habit.

Now let's use these difficulties to create our simple fitness plan.

A SIMPLE FITNESS PLAN

What we want is a plan that isn't difficult to adopt, and even more importantly, is something you can stick with for years. It might not get you instant results, but those aren't the results you want anyway. Any plan that gets you dramatic results within a short time is a bad plan, because it is too drastic, and no one can stick with a drastic plan for very long. Soon, you fall off such a drastic plan, and those dramatic results you achieved are reversed in just as dramatic a fashion.

Real health and fitness come over a period of months and years. Lasting change is made gradually, in small increments, in a way that you can sustain for life. And so our plan will be something that will start out slowly, but will be sustainable for much longer than more drastic plans.

Conventional wisdom says that diet is about 80 percent of weight loss, and to a large extent that's true, because you can lose weight with a good diet and no exercise, but it's really hard to lose weight on a bad diet with exercise. But we're going to turn that on its head for two reasons: 1) We're not just looking to lose weight, but to get fit and in good shape, and for that you need both exercise and diet; and 2) If you start out with exercise, the diet will eventually follow. It's hard to exercise without at least wanting to eat right, so we're going to start with exercise.

So our simple fitness plan is this:

1. Use the first month to focus exclusively on forming the exercise habit. Don't worry about the diet at this point, although you can start eating healthier foods if you like. But the habit of exercise is our focus: We want to make it as regular and as important as brushing our teeth. We will start small and focus on making it a regular thing, rather than going all out this first month.

2. The second month, while continuing the exercise habit, we'll focus on making gradual, healthy changes to our diet.

3. Every month thereafter, we will set short-term goals for gradual improvements in our exercise and diet plans. We will reward ourselves each month for our progress, and stay accountable to others for our fitness plan.

STEP 1: FORMING THE EXERCISE HABIT

Forming the exercise habit doesn't have to be a monumental task. It's like forming any other habit—you just need to be consistent about it. The Spanish have a proverb, that habits start out as cobwebs and grow to be cables. So we will start out by laying thin strings, and gradually add to those strings until we have cables.

Of course, if you have any health risks, such as heart or lung problems or serious illness or pregnancy, please check with a doctor before starting any exercise program.

Here's the plan:

1. **Start light.** Start your workout plan as easy as possible until you've learned to stick to it. You can gradually increase your exercise later, but at first it is vitally important that you hold yourself back. The first week, just do five to ten minutes of cardio—fast walking, running, cycling, or swimming. Only five to ten minutes, and no more. You will want to do more, most likely, but don't. The next week, increase your time by five minutes, and do that every week for the first month, so that by the end of the month you're doing twenty to twenty-five minutes each workout. If this seems like too little to you, don't

worry; after it becomes a habit you can do more. Focus on forming the habit first.

2. **Schedule your workout time.** This is crucial—figure out a time when you will be able to exercise, when nothing will interfere. For most people, morning is the best time, because evening workouts are often canceled due to social engagements or other obligations. But for some people, working out right after work is best, and for others, a lunchtime workout works well. Choose the time that works best for you, and create space in your schedule for your workouts. The first week, you just need to schedule three workouts—give yourself thirty minutes, as the workout appointment always takes longer than the workout itself. The second and third weeks, schedule four workouts, and the fourth week, schedule five workouts. Try to stay with five workouts a week from then on, as this is the best way to get in good shape. This is important: Treat these workout appointments as your most important appointments of the day. Don't let anything get in the way of them.

3. **Don't allow yourself to miss a day.** Just about the only good reasons to miss a workout are sickness or injury. Otherwise, don't let yourself skip a workout. These workouts are so light, in the beginning, that they shouldn't be tiring you out too much. If you're tired from a long day's work, just start the workout—you'll be glad you did. If you start skipping workouts, you will soon make a habit of not exercising, instead of the

other way around. When forming a habit, it's very important that you be consistent. Remember, it's just like brushing your teeth—do it for your health, do it regularly, and just do it.

4. **Don't give up.** Even more important than not missing a day is sticking with the program. If for some reason you do miss a day or two, don't stop. Get back on the program. If you miss more than a couple of days, back up the program a week or two and start working on forming the habit again. If you get discouraged and stop, motivate yourself and start again. Failure is not as important as starting again after you fail, and sticking with it for the long term.

5. **Get a partner if you can.** This isn't mandatory, but if you can find a reliable partner, it makes it a bit easier. First, having someone to talk to while you exercise makes the time go by much more quickly. Second, if you make an appointment to meet that person for your workout, you're more likely to stick to the appointment rather than wimp out.

6. **Be accountable to others.** This is how you motivate yourself to stick with the program—no one wants to look bad in front of others. Commit publicly, to your friends or to the entire world via a blog, to stick with the program. Keep a strict workout and eating log, and make it public. Share it with as many people as possible. Let the light shine where once there was darkness, and that accountability will motivate you.

7. **Enjoy yourself.** Very mandatory. If you don't enjoy yourself, you'll never stick with it. So try to have as much fun as possible. Enjoy getting fit and healthy! Enjoy burning off your fat! Enjoy the sweat! Enjoy the relaxation of burning off stress! Exercise should be fun, not torture.

That's the plan to form the exercise habit. It's pretty simple actually—create the time to work out, start easy, and stick with it without fail. Soon, exercise will become such a regular part of your life you'll never want to go back to being sedentary again.

STEP 2: MAKING GRADUAL HEALTHY DIET CHANGES

After your month of forming the exercise habit, it's time to start focusing on your eating habits. If you already eat fairly healthily, you can modify this to suit your needs, and try to make further improvements in your diet gradually. If you don't eat too healthily now, you don't want to make drastic changes—small, gradual changes over time are better and more sustainable.

Here's your plan:

1. **Eat when you're lightly hungry.** Not when you're ravenous. That means eating every three to four hours and paying more attention to your hunger. If you're getting hungry, eat. Action steps: Plan meals every three to four hours, be more aware of your hunger, pack snacks or meals for on the road. This is

your plan for the first week—don't worry about the next steps until after the first week.

2. **Eat light foods.** Nothing too heavy, except cheat meals (schedule this once a week). Lots of fruits and veggies, whole grains, beans, and nuts. Fresh food much better than processed. Action steps: Make a list of healthy meals and snacks with real, whole foods—things you like that are healthy. Turn them into meal plans—several days' worth of meals and snacks. You'll start on this the second week, but don't change your entire diet overnight. This week, just try eating more fruits and veggies, or cut out sodas and other sweet drinks. The next week, make another change, perhaps eliminating some junk food you eat regularly, or cooking a healthier dinner. Aim to gradually have a diet that consists of very little junk food or fast food, and mostly combinations of the following: fruits and veggies, beans, nuts, whole grains, low-fat dairy or soy milk products, and lean protein (lean meat, chicken, fish, tofu, or other vegetable protein). Be sure to find foods you enjoy eating, or you'll have a difficult time—this is very important.

3. **Eat slowly.** Savor the food. Don't cram it down. Eating slowly will help you not to get overfull, and will help you enjoy your food more. Focus on this step in the third week while continuing the first two steps.

4. **Eat until you're lightly full. Not stuffed.** Stop before you're really full, and wait ten minutes to see if you're really still

hungry. This is a crucial step, and you'll focus on it in the fourth week while continuing the progress you've made in the first few weeks.

No dieting, no restricted foods, all good stuff. This plan is really about learning how to eat healthier, and to feel lighter all the time. Remember to take it one step at a time!

STEP 3: CONTINUATION, SHORT-TERM GOALS AND ACCOUNTABILITY

Now that you've gotten started with the habits of exercise and healthy eating, you'll want to continue the program and gradually improve both areas. This can be a dangerous time for many people, as they lose motivation if they don't see big results. So to keep you from losing motivation, and to keep you sticking to the program to see the long-term results, we'll do the following:

1. **Continue to gradually increase exercise, adding variety.** Crank it up, but only slowly. Once you've gotten used to exercise, you'll want to first lengthen your workouts to thirty to forty minutes, and then do some higher intensity ones for better fitness and fat-burning. For example, instead of running slowly and steadily, for a long time, try doing shorter bursts of fast running, with periods of rest in between. You can do this for any exercise. Higher intensity increases the calorie burn, and improves performance. But you can't do it as long, and you shouldn't do it every workout. Mix it in with endurance workouts. Also try signing up for a 5K or other type of short race—it adds motivation and fun.

2. **Continue to eat healthier, also adding variety and flavor.** Each week, make one healthy change to your diet. Try out a new healthy recipe. Pack healthy snacks for work. Pack healthy lunches for work. Eat a healthier breakfast. Eat out less and cook more. Pack healthy snacks when you go out on the road. Drink more water. Cut out some type of unhealthy food. One by one, change your eating habits to healthier ones. Doing it gradually like this makes it much easier and much more likely to stick. To add variety, be sure to try out new recipes and new fruits and veggies and snacks, and when you find ones you like, add them to your regular rotation. Never stop trying new healthy foods and recipes!

3. **Set short-term goals.** Real, lasting change only happens over a long period of time—months and years. But it's hard to stay motivated for something that long. Instead, set a short-term goal or two each month. Maybe set a goal each week if that helps. Some examples of short-term goals: Increase your workouts by five minutes each day this week. Lose a pound a week. Lose an inch off your waist. Run a 5K. Get your total workout time to two-and-a-half hours this week. Do a long run of five miles on Saturday. As you can see, the possibilities for short-term goals are almost endless. Set one every week or two to keep yourself motivated. Share your goals with others.

4. **Hold yourself accountable. Log your eating and exercise daily.** This is the key habit. If you can log your workout, you will start to see your progress, and it will motivate you to

keep going. And you have to make it a habit to log it right away. Don't put it off and say you'll do it before you go to bed. As soon as you're done working out, log it. No exceptions. And don't make the log complicated—that will only make you resist doing the log. Just the date, time, and what you did. This is also important: Put your log online, on a blog or through one of many online logs available, so that others can see what you've been doing. Give the address of your log to as many people as you can, and encourage them to check on it and leave comments. The accountability will keep you motivated to keep going.

5. **Reward yourself.** Rewards are best if they are frequent in the beginning. Be self-indulgent! Even sweets are good rewards—get into the habit of exercise, and weight loss will come eventually. Celebrate every little success.

30 EXERCISE MOTIVATIONS

There are a million ways to motivate yourself to exercise, actually, but these are a few that seem to work very well.

1. **How you feel after a workout.** A good workout is an amazing feeling. Remember that feeling and let it motivate you before your next workout.

2. **Time for you.** While many people make time to take care of others (kids, spouse, other family, coworkers, boss), they

don't often make time to take care of themselves. Instead, make your "you" time a priority, and don't miss that exercise appointment.

3. **Calories burned.** If you count calories (and it's really one of the most effective ways to lose weight), you know that the more you exercise, the more calories you burn—and the bigger your calorie deficit.

4. **Having fun.** Exercise should be fun. If it isn't, try a different kind of activity that you enjoy. As long as you're moving, it's good for you.

5. **How you're going to look.** Imagine a slimmer, fitter you. Now let that visualization drive you.

6. **Magazines.** It's very motivational to read fitness magazines. When you read about something, you want to do it.

7. **Cover models.** Sure, they're genetically freaky, and probably Photoshopped to look perfect. But for some reason, looking at how good a cover model looks helps motivate people to work harder.

8. **Blogs.** It's fun to read blogs about people who are into exercising, or losing weight. It can show the ups and downs they go through, and you can learn from their experiences.

9. **Success stories.** The success stories of others are incredibly inspirational. If a fitness Web site has success stories, make it a point to read them.

10. **Forums.** Do the monthly challenge on the Zen Habits forums (http://zenhabits.net/forums/), or join another forum full of like-minded peopled. Check in daily. It really helps.

11. **Fitting into new clothes.** Want to look good in a smaller size? Work out!

12. **Being attractive.** That's always a good motivator, as we all know.

13. **Adrenaline rush.** There is a rush when you exercise. Ride that rush to complete the workout.

14. **Stress relief.** Wound up after a long day at the office? Get out and work off that stress. It makes a world of difference.

15. **Time for contemplation.** The quiet time of exercise is perfect for thinking about anything going on in your life.

16. **A workout partner.** One of the best motivators ever.

17. **An exercise class.** Sign up for a class, perhaps with a friend, and you'll be motivated to get there and work out.

18. **A coach or trainer.** Worth the money, just for the motivation.

19. **An exercise log/graph.** For some reason, writing it down is extremely important. Do it for a week and you'll see the power of the log.

20. **Your before picture.** You often don't realize how far you've come. Take pictures.

21. **A 5K race or triathlon.** Just sign up for one and you'll be motivated to train.

22. **The dread of feeling "yuck" from not exercising.** I hate how I feel after not exercising. So I remind myself of that when I feel tired.

23. **Living long enough to see your grandkids** . . . and play with them.

24. **The scale.** It's not motivating to weigh yourself every day, as your weight fluctuates. But if you weigh yourself once a week, you'll be motivated to have it keep going down, instead of up. Combine the scale with the measuring tape, and measure your waist.

25. **Reaching a goal.** Set a goal for weight, or your waist measurement, or a number of days to work out, or a number of

miles to run this week. Setting and tracking a goal helps motivate you to complete that goal. Make it easily achievable.

26. **Posting it on your blog.** Tell people you're going to lose weight or exercise daily, and report to them. You'll make it happen.

27. **Motivational quotes.** Print out your favorite motivational quotes or put them on your computer desktop.

28. **Books.** Buy fitness or healthy cookbooks as a reward. You'll get a renewed sense of purpose.

29. **Others commenting on how good you look.** When someone notices the changes in your body, it feels good. And it makes you want to work out more.

30. **An upcoming day at the beach, or a reunion.** You can't help but want to look good.

eighteen

On Motivation

ONE OF THE biggest challenges in meeting any goal, whether it be related to productivity, waking early, changing a habit, exercising, or just becoming happier, is finding the motivation to stick with it. This chapter is designed to help you meet the goals and build the habits of the rest of this book—look at it as a keystone to all the other principles presented here.

If you can stick with a goal long enough, you'll get there. It just takes patience and motivation.

Motivation is the key, but it's not always easy, day in and day out, to find that motivation. What follows is a guide to motivation for anything you try to achieve using this book, because there will always be points along your journey to success where your motivation will falter, and you'll feel like giving up. Don't quit. Sticking with something for the long term is the true path to anything worthwhile.

HOW DOES MOTIVATION WORK?

Before we get into specific methods, it's useful to examine what motivation is, what it does, and how it works.

Motivation is what drives you toward a goal, what keeps you going when things get tough, the reason you get up early to exercise or work late to finish a project. There are all kinds of motivations, of course, from positive to negative. Having a boss threaten to fire you is motivation—you're likely to work harder to complete a project with that kind of pressure. But I find that positive motivation works better.

So motivation, in its best form, is a way for you to want to do something. There may be times, for example, when you don't feel like getting up early, and in those times you may just want to sleep in (not that there's anything wrong with that). But if you have a reason to want to get up early, something you really want to do, you'll jump up out of bed with excitement.

The best kind of motivation, then, is for you to really want something, to get excited about it, to be passionate about it. Remember that, as there are many other types of motivation (especially negative), but in my experience, this is the kind that works the best. There is only so long that you can go on trying to motivate yourself to do something you don't like to do, something you don't want to do. But if you find ways to really want to do something, you can sustain your effort for long enough to achieve your goal.

8 WAYS TO MOTIVATE YOURSELF FROM THE BEGINNING

It's important to start out with the right motivation, because a good start can build momentum that you can sustain for a long time. If you start out right, you have a much better chance of succeeding. Here are some tips for starting out:

1. **Start small.** I've said this before, but that's because it's one of the most important tips in motivating yourself toward a goal. Don't start out big! Start out with a ridiculously easy goal, and then grow from there.

2. **One goal.** Too many people start with too many goals at once, and try to do too much. And it saps energy and motivation. It's probably the most common mistake that people make. You have to choose one goal, for now, and focus on it completely.

3. **Examine your motivation.** Know your reasons. Give them some thought . . . and write them down. If you have loved ones, and you are doing it for them, that is more powerful than just doing it for self-interest. Doing it for yourself is good too, but you should do it for something that you really want to happen, for really good reasons.

4. **Really, really want it.** This is essentially the same as the above tip, but I want to emphasize it: It's not enough to think it would be cool to achieve something. It has to be something you're passionate about, something you're super excited about, something you want deeply. Make sure that your goal meets these criteria, or you won't stick with it for long.

5. **Commit publicly.** None of us likes to look bad in front of others. We will go the extra mile to do something we've said publicly.

6. **Get excited.** Well, it starts with inspiration from others (see above), but you have to take that excitement and build on it. For me, I've learned that by talking to my wife about it, and to others, and reading as much about it as possible, and visualizing what it would be like to be successful (seeing the benefits of the goal in my head), I get excited about a goal. Once I've done that, it's just a matter of carrying that energy forward and keeping it going.

7. **Build anticipation.** This will sound hard, and many people will skip this tip. But it really works. It helped me quit smoking after many failed attempts. If you find inspiration and want to achieve a goal, don't start right away. Many of us will get excited and want to start today. That's a mistake. Set a date in the future—a week or two, or even a month—and make that your Start Date. Mark it on the calendar. Get excited about that date. Make it the most important date in your life. By delaying your

start, you are building anticipation, and increasing your focus and energy for your goal.

8. **Print it out, post it up.** Print out your goal in big words. Make your goal just a few words long, like a mantra ("Exercise 15 mins. Daily"), and post it up on your wall or refrigerator. Post it at home and work. Put it on your computer desktop. You want to have big reminders about your goal, to keep your focus and keep your excitement going. A picture of your goal (like a model with sexy abs, for example) also helps.

20 WAYS TO SUSTAIN MOTIVATION WHEN YOU'RE STRUGGLING

The second half of motivation is to keep yourself going when you don't feel the same excitement as you did in the beginning. Perhaps something new has come into your life and your old goal isn't as much of a priority anymore. Perhaps you skipped a day or two and now you can't get back into it. Perhaps you screwed up and got discouraged.

If you can get yourself excited again, and keep going, you'll get there, eventually. But if you give up, you won't. It's your choice—accomplish the goal, or quit. Here's how you can stop from quitting, and get to your goal:

1. **Hold yourself back.** When we start a new exercise program, or any new goal really, we are usually raring to go. We are full of excitement, and our enthusiasm knows no boundaries.

Nor does our sense of self-limitation. We think we can do anything. It's not long, though, before we learn that we do have limitations, and our enthusiasm begins to wane. Well, a great motivator when you have so much energy at the beginning of a program, and want to go all out is—to hold yourself back! Don't let yourself do everything you want to do. Only let yourself do 50 to 75 percent of what you want to do. And plan out a course of action where you slowly increase over time. For example, if I want to go running, I might think I can run three miles at first. But instead of letting myself do that, I start by only running one mile. When I'm running that mile, I'll be telling myself that I can do more! But I don't let myself. After that workout, I'll be looking forward to the next workout, when I'll let myself do a mile and a half. I keep that energy reined in, harness it, so that I can ride it even further.

2. **Just start.** There are some days when you don't feel like heading out the door for a run, or figuring out your budget, or whatever it is you're supposed to do that day for your goal. Well, instead of thinking about how hard it is, and how long it will take, tell yourself that you just have to start. I have a rule that I just have to put on my running shoes and close the door behind me. After that, it all flows naturally. It's when you're sitting in your house, thinking about running and feeling tired, that it seems hard. Once you start, it is never as hard as you thought it would be. This tip works for me every time.

3. **Stay accountable.** If you committed yourself publicly, through an online forum, on a blog, by e-mail, or in person . . .

stay accountable to that group of people. Commit to report back to them daily, or something like that, and stick to it! That accountability will help you to want to do well, because you don't want to report that you've failed.

4. **Squash negative thoughts and replace them with positive ones.** This is one of the most important motivation skills, and I suggest you practice it daily. It's important to start monitoring your thoughts, and to recognize negative self-talk. Just spend a few days becoming aware of every negative thought. Then, after a few days, try squashing those negative thoughts like a bug, and replacing them with a corresponding positive thought. Squash, "This is too hard!" and replace it with, "I can do this! If that wimp Leo can do it, so can I!" It sounds corny, but it works. Really.

5. **Think about the benefits.** Thinking about how hard something is is a big problem for most people. Waking early sounds so hard! Just thinking about it makes you tired. But instead of thinking about how hard something is, think about what you will get out of it. For example, instead of thinking about how hard it is to wake early, focus on how good you'll feel when you're done, and how your day will be so much better. The benefits of something will help energize you.

6. **Get excited again!** Think about why you lost your excitement . . . then think about why you were excited in the first place. Can you get that back? What made you want to do the

goal? What made you passionate about it? Try to build that up again, refocus yourself, get energized.

7. **Read about it.** When I lose motivation, I just read a book or blog about my goal. It inspires me and reinvigorates me. For some reason, reading helps motivate and focus you on whatever you're reading about. So read about your goal every day, if you can, especially when you're not feeling motivated.

8. **Find like-minded friends.** Staying motivated on your own is tough. But if you find someone with similar goals (running, dieting, finances, etc.), see if they'd like to partner with you. Or partner with your spouse, sibling, or best friend on whatever goals they're trying to achieve. You don't have to be going after the same goals—as long as you are both pushing and encouraging each other to succeed. Other good options are groups in your area (I'm part of a running club, for example) or online forums where you can find people to talk to about your goals.

9. **Read inspiring stories.** Inspiration, for me, comes from others who have achieved what I want to achieve, or who are currently doing it. I read other blogs, books, magazines. I Google my goal, and read success stories. Zen Habits is just one place for inspiration, not only from me but from many readers who have achieved amazing things. I love, love, love reading success stories too.

10. **Build on your successes.** Every little step along the way is a success—celebrate the fact that you even started! And then did it for two days! Celebrate every little milestone. Then take that successful feeling and build on it with another baby step. Add two to three minutes to your exercise routine, for example. With each step (and each step should last about a week), you will feel even more successful. Make each step really, really small, and you won't fail. After a couple of months, your tiny steps will add up to a lot of progress and a lot of success.

11. **Just get through the low points.** Motivation is not a constant thing that is always there for you. It comes and goes, and comes and goes again, like the tide. But realize that while it may go away, it doesn't do so permanently. It will come back. Just stick it out and wait for that motivation to come back. In the meantime, read about your goal, ask for help, and do some of the other things listed here until your motivation comes back.

12. **Get help.** It's hard to accomplish something alone. When I decided to run my marathon, I had the help of friends and family, and I had a great running community on Guam who encouraged me at 5K races and did long runs with me. When I decided to quit smoking, I joined an online forum and that helped tremendously. And of course, my wife, Eva, helped every step of the way. I couldn't have reached these goals without her, or without the others who supported me. Find your support network, either in the real world or online, or both.

13. **Chart your progress.** This can be as simple as marking an X on your calendar or creating a simple spreadsheet, or logging your goal using online software. But it can be vastly rewarding to look back on your progress and to see how far you've come, and it can help you to keep going—you don't want to have too many days without an X! Now, you will have some bad marks on your chart. That's OK. Don't let a few bad marks stop you from continuing. Strive instead to get the good marks next time.

14. **Reward yourself often.** For every little step along the way, celebrate your success, and give yourself a reward. It helps to write down appropriate rewards for each step, so that you can look forward to those rewards. By appropriate, I mean 1) it's proportionate to the size of the goal (don't reward going on a one-mile run with a luxury cruise in the Bahamas); and 2) it doesn't ruin your goal—if you are trying to lose weight, don't reward a day of healthy eating with a dessert binge. It's self-defeating.

15. **Go for mini-goals.** Sometimes large or longer-term goals can be overwhelming. After a couple weeks, we may lose motivation, because we still have several months or a year or more left to accomplish the goal. It's hard to maintain motivation for a single goal for such a long time. Solution: Have smaller goals along the way.

16. **Get a coach or take a class.** These will motivate you to at least show up and to take action. They can be applied to any goal. This might be one of the more expensive ways of motivat-

ing yourself, but it works. And if you do some research, you might find some cheap classes in your area, or you might know a friend who will provide coaching or counseling for free.

17. **Never skip two days in a row.** This rule takes into account our natural tendency to miss days now and then. We are not perfect. So, you missed one day . . . now the second day is upon you and you are feeling lazy. Tell yourself, "No! You will not miss two days in a row!"

18. **Use visualization.** Visualize your successful outcome in great detail. Close your eyes and think about exactly how your successful outcome will look, will feel, will smell and taste and sound. Where are you when you become successful? How do you look? What are you wearing? Form as clear a mental picture as possible. Now here's the next key: Do it every day. For at least a few minutes each day. This is the only way to keep that motivation going over a long period of time.

19. **Be aware of your urges to quit, and overcome them.** We all have urges to stop, but they are mostly unconscious. One of the most powerful things you can do is to start being more conscious of those urges. A good exercise is to go through the day with a little piece of paper and put a tally mark for each time you get an urge. It simply makes you aware of the urges. Then have a plan for when those urges hit, and plan for it beforehand—and write down your plan, because once those urges hit, you will not feel like coming up with a plan.

20. **Find pleasure again.** No one can stick to something for long if they find it unpleasant and are only rewarded after months of toil. There has to be fun, pleasure, joy in it, every day, or you won't want to do it. Find those pleasurable things—the beauty of a morning run, for example, or the satisfaction in reporting to people that you finished another step along the way, or the deliciousness of a healthy meal.

ACKNOWLEDGMENTS

I'd like to acknowledge the invaluable help of the many people who contributed to this book, including Holly and Brendan, who had great patience for this first-time author. The readers of Zen Habits inspired and encouraged me every step of the way. My mom, Shannon, who has been the rock upon which my life has been built. My father, Joe, whose wit and humor have infused everything I do. My sister Katrina, who is both my running partner and confidant, and my beautiful sisters Ana and Tiara, and my wonderful brothers Joseph, Brandon, and Austin. My incredible children, the reasons for everything I do: Chloe, Justin, Rain, Maia, Seth, and Noelle.

And of course my wife, Eva, my greatest supporter.

Notes

Notes

Notes

Notes

Hay House Titles of Related Interest

Ask and It Is Given, by Esther and Jerry Hicks

Return to the Sacred, by Jonathan H. Ellerby

Spent, by Frank Lipman

You Can Have What You Want, by Michael Neill

Anxiety Free, by Robert L. Leahy

Being in Balance, by Wayne W. Dyer PhD

Life Lessons, by Lesley Garner

Lucid Living, by Timothy Freke

We hope you enjoyed this Hay House book.
If you would like to receive a free catalogue featuring additional
Hay House books and products, or if you would like information
about the Hay Foundation, please contact:

Hay House UK Ltd
292B Kensal Road • London W10 5BE
Tel: (44) 20 8962 1230; Fax: (44) 20 8962 1239
www.hayhouse.co.uk
***

Published and distributed in Australia by:
Hay House Australia Ltd • 18/36 Ralph Street • Alexandria, NSW 2015
Tel: (61) 2 9669 4299, Fax: (61) 2 9669 4144
www.hayhouse.com.au
***

Published and distributed in the Republic of South Africa by:
Hay House SA (Pty) Ltd • PO Box 990 • Witkoppen 2068
Tel/Fax: (27) 11 467 8904
www.hayhouse.co.za
***

Published and distributed in India by:
Hay House Publishers India • Muskaan Complex • Plot No.3
B-2• Vasant Kunj • New Delhi - 110 070
Tel: (91) 11 41761620; Fax: (91) 11 41761630
www.hayhouse.co.in

***

Sign up via the Hay House UK website to receive the Hay House
online newsletter and stay informed about what's going on with your
favourite authors. You'll receive bimonthly announcements
about discounts and offers, special events, product highlights,
free excerpts, giveaways, and more!
www.hayhouse.co.uk

JOIN THE HAY HOUSE FAMILY

As the leading self-help, mind, body and spirit publisher in the UK, we'd like to welcome you to our family so that you can enjoy all the benefits our website has to offer.

 EXTRACTS from a selection of your favourite author titles

 COMPETITIONS, PRIZES & SPECIAL OFFERS Win extracts, money off, downloads and so much more

 LISTEN to a range of radio interviews and our latest audio publications

 CELEBRATE YOUR BIRTHDAY An inspiring gift will be sent your way

 LATEST NEWS Keep up with the latest news from and about our Authors

 ATTEND OUR AUTHOR EVENTS Be the first to hear about our author events

 iPHONE APPS Download your favourite app for your iPhone

 HAY HOUSE INFORMATION Ask us anything, all enquiries answered

join us online at **www.hayhouse.co.uk**

 HAY HOUSE 292B Kensal Road, London W10 5BE
T: 020 8962 1230 E: info@hayhouse.co.uk